small

gardens

small
gardens

DAVID SQUIRE

p

This is a Parragon Book
This edition published in 2006

Parragon
Queen Street House
4 Queen Street
Bath BA1 1HE, UK

Produced by The Bridgewater Book Company Ltd.

ISBN: 1-40546-380-5

Printed in China

NOTE
For growing and harvesting, calendar information applies
only to the Northern Hemisphere (US zones 5–9).

contents

introduction

Few gardens are large and nowadays most are less than the size of a tennis court. But whatever the size it is possible to grow plants in an imaginative way that creates an outdoor area for family living. Climbers on free-standing trellises are superb for providing privacy and spectacular displays of flowers and leaves, while plants in window boxes and hanging baskets decorate walls and windows; those in tubs and planters create colour at patio level. Many small gardens do not have a lawn and this clearly eliminates the need to buy, house and maintain a mower. However, an ornamental lawn-type feature can be created from chamomile and a decorative path from thyme. Both do not have the hard wearing nature of grass, but in a small area produce exciting features that are sure to capture attention.

Inspirational yet practical

This all-colour book is packed with practical information about both improving an existing garden and a brand new one, perhaps surrounded by a sea of rubble left by the builders of the new house. Assessing and improving soil is described, as well as gardening on slopes and dealing with varying amounts of light and shade. A wide range of paths for small gardens, as well as walls, fences and steps, is described so that the right one can be selected. And, of course, a firm-surfaced patio, terrace or courtyard is essential; much of the pleasure derived from a garden is to use it as an outdoor living area. Pergolas, arches, trellises, arbours, flowering tunnels and porches are other important features and their range and use are thoroughly detailed. All gardeners have a preference for specific garden features and these range from lawns that enable children and animals to play safely, to water gardens, thyme paths, rock gardens, groups of fragrant plants and, or course, a vast range of roses from bush types to ramblers and climbers. These are all covered, with advice on how to integrate them into a garden.

▲ Whether in sunlight or shade a border can become awash with colourful flowers and attractive leaves. There are plants for all places.

HEIGHTS AND SPREADS

The heights and spreads given for shrubs and trees refer to 15–20-year-old specimens growing in good conditions. Eventually, these plants may grow even larger.

Using plants in a garden

In a small garden it is essential to plan the positions of plants so that they give the best possible display. Colour-themed gardens, perhaps dominant in pink-and-red, blue-and-purple, yellow-and-gold and white-and-silver are popular, while those with variegated foliage remain attractive over a long period. More frequently, plants are grown in mixed-colour borders, where flowers of all hues and shapes jostle side by side to form a traditional English flower border. To create an even more impressive display from single-colour themes, position them against colour-enhancing backgrounds provided by hedges, such as yew and other conifers. Window boxes and hanging baskets can also be given this added design quality by positioning them against colour-washed walls. Growing your own food is important and fresh salad plants are possible in even the smallest garden. Tomatoes and lettuces grow well in growing-bags, while herbs are ideal for planting in ornamental pots and planters. There are even planters with cup-like holes in their sides that enable a wide range of small herbs to be grown in a confined area. Additionally, containers help to restrain the invasive nature of mints that after a few years often become a nuisance in a herb border. Dwarf rootstocks now enable apples to be grown in large tubs on a patio, while both apples and pears can be grown as espaliers or cordons near to a wall or in a narrow bed perhaps alongside a path. Peaches, nectarines and plums can be grown in fan-shaped forms against walls and strong fences that are sheltered and in full sun.

▲ *Achillea is an ideal herbaceous perennial for growing in a dry, sunny border. Its flowers are ideal for cutting and displaying indoors.*

▼ *Plants with variegated leaves create colour throughout summer and, if evergreen, the entire year. Many can be grown in pots and tubs.*

design inspirations

The choice of styles for your garden is wide and these range from English flower gardens to patios and courtyards which are ideal for creating outdoor living areas in space-restricted places. Pergolas, arches and trellises can be used to create height as well as to provide seclusion and mystery, while arbours add romanticism to a garden. Paths, steps, walls and fences are essential garden features and with careful planning these can be attractive as well as functional.

making the most of your soil

Soil can be slowly improved by adding well-decayed manure or garden compost, but more instant ways to create a colourful garden are to select plants that survive the conditions in your garden. It is inevitable, however, that gardeners will wish to grow other kinds of plants.

Raised beds

Where the ground is continually moist and drainage is difficult, or if the soil is exceptionally chalky or acid, construct a raised bed 30–45cm/12–18in high and fill it with good soil. This enables a wealth of plants to be grown. Use cascading plants at the sides so that the edges are cloaked.

Preparing planting areas

Where the soil is exceptionally dry or of poor quality, small areas can be improved to enable climbers and other plants to be grown. Dig out the soil from an area about 60cm/2ft square and deep, and fill the lower 10cm/4in with rubble. Top up with good top-soil and firm it. Put in the plant and, until established, water the area regularly. Do not plant climbers less than 30cm/1ft from a wall, where the soil will be quite dry.

Growing acid-loving plants

Soils that are only slightly acid can be improved by dusting the surface with hydrated lime or ground limestone each winter. This applies to most soils, but where it is strongly acid and mainly formed of peat substitute, it is better to grow acid-loving plants such as callunas and heathers. There are many varieties, and some are known for their flowers while others have attractive foliage. Where the area is lightly shaded and the

◄ *Where there is a problem with the soil, a raised bed is an ideal solution. Additionally, it enables plants to be easily seen and reached.*

soil slightly acid, azaleas create a spectacular display in spring.

Growing chalk-loving plants

It is more difficult to correct chalky soil than acid types. Acidic fertilizers such as sulphate of ammonia can be used, with additions of peat sustitute, but if the underlying nature is alkaline it is better to grow chalk-loving plants. For gardeners with acid soil and an unsuppressible desire to grow chalk-loving plants, a raised bed is the best solution.

Wet and boggy areas

Many soils with a high water level can be drained, enabling a wide range of plants to be grown. However, if the area is naturally wet, difficult to drain and perhaps close to a stream, it is better to plant moisture-loving plants. They include *Lysichiton americanus* (skunk cabbage) with bright yellow, arum-like flower heads in spring and its near relative *Lysichiton camtschatcensis*, with pure white flowers. Along the sides of streams plant shrubs such as *Cornus stolonifera* 'Flaviramea' for its coloured winter stems.

Hot and dry soils

Gardening on hot and dry soils very much depends on three factors: annually mixing in bulky materials such as well-rotted manure and garden compost to aid water retention, regular watering and adding a mulch each spring. Selecting plants that survive hot and dry soil is also important (see pages 42–43).

Pots, tubs and other containers

Where the soil is so inhospitable that plants cannot be easily grown, the answer is a wide array of plants in containers. They range from pots and tubs to window boxes, hanging baskets, troughs and wall baskets. Buying, planting and looking after plants in containers is more expensive and involves more work than caring for plants in borders and beds. However, it does provide you with the opportunity to change and recreate your garden as often as you wish, which can be an advantage.

▲ To bring colour throughout the year, plant large pots with dwarf or slow-growing conifers and position them along the edges of a path.

▼ Cloak the sides of natural stone walls with plants, growing in the wall or planted at the base. Alternatively, use attractive pots of plants.

gardening on slopes

Sloping ground offers an opportunity to create an unusual garden, but clearly it will be more expensive than developing a flat site. A series of paved, terraced areas around a house make an attractive feature when the ground slopes downwards from the house.

▲ *A paved area, halfway up a slope, creates an exciting yet practical leisure area, especially when a pond and fountain are a feature.*

Terraced gardens

Terraced gardens can be formal or informal partly depending on the style of the house. Modern houses usually demand formal terraces connected by flights of steps. Cottages, especially in rural settings, perhaps with a slope dotted with fruit trees, require informality.

Paved areas

When a house is at the bottom of a facing slope, a flat, paved area can usually be constructed at its base, but also consider creating a paved area about one-third of the way up the slope to break up the degree of incline. Where possible, position the area so that it can be seen from the ground floor of the house without people having to crick their necks unduly.

Where the ground falls away from the house, construct a flat, paved area as near to the house as possible. Meandering paths can then lead downwards from it, perhaps criss-crossing the slope to make them appear less steep and easier to use. These paved areas need not be central but towards one side, which particularly suits informal gardens. Where the end of a garden rises, construct a paved area and erect a summer house on top. Check that the neighbours will not think it an intrusion on their privacy.

Retaining walls

They are invariably constructed across slopes to retain banks of soil up to 1.2m/4ft high. Some walls are formal while others are made of natural stone, and are used to plant up *Aurinia saxatilis* (still better known as *Alyssum saxatile*) and aubretia. By positioning wide paths along the base of informal retaining walls the plants can be appreciated without being damaged. Formal retaining walls, especially when made of brick, do not need a wide path alongside them. However, if a lawn is positioned close to them, construct a mowing strip at the base to enable a lawn mower to cut close to the wall.

Sloping woodland and wild gardens

Old railway sleepers are ideal for retaining soil on steep slopes in rustic areas. Secure the sleepers in position, using strong wooden posts or metal spikes. Beds of heathers and deciduous azaleas create superb displays on slopes. Logs can also be used to restrain soil and to create an attractive and natural edging that especially harmonizes with informal gardens. Use several strong, wooden stakes to secure them in position and pack well-drained, friable soil along the inside edge.

Lawn banks

Traditionally, especially on large country estates, slopes were terraced and grassed, with 45-degree slopes separating level areas 3–3.6m/10–12ft wide. These dramatic features can easily be replicated on a smaller scale in formal gardens. The key is to keep it all in proportion.

▲ *Flights of steps create visually exciting features in gardens. Ensure that they are soundly constructed and have all-weather surfaces.*

◀ *Slopes are ideal places for a series of waterfalls. If they are extensive it may be necessary to have a reservoir tank at the top.*

aspect, light and shade

The range of trees, shrubs, herbaceous perennials, annuals and other garden plants is wide, and there are types for all aspects and intensities of light or shade. Some of these extremes can be lessened by planting or cutting down trees, but usually it is a matter of learning to live with your garden.

◄ *Whether in sunlight or shade a border can become awash with colourful flowers and attractive leaves. There are plants for all places.*

The lottery of aspect

A garden's aspect is not usually the first consideration when buying a house. Rather, it is one of the lotteries of gardening. Cold, searing wind is a problem for some plants, while strong, intense sunlight causes difficulties for many. There are possibilities and limitations in all gardens; there are plants for even the most inhospitable places. Within this book there are many ideas that will make growing plants easy. For example, plants for hot sun are described on pages 42–43, and those for shade on pages 44–45.

Coastal considerations

Coastal gardens are at risk from several factors. Cold, strong, buffeting winds may deform trees and shrubs, especially in winter, and the salt-laden wind will damage leaves and flowers. Creating windbreaks and hedges to filter the wind and reduce its speed is essential, especially when close to the sea. However, there are plenty of strong, hardy plants to choose from.

Winter wonderlands

In some areas, winter weather is so harsh that the likelihood of flowers is dramatically reduced. However, several hardy trees flower during winter and they include *Hamamelis mollis* (Chinese witch hazel) and *Cornus mas* (Cornelian cherry). Additionally, frost forms attractive patterns on leaves, while a light dusting of snow creates a further feature.

In exceptionally cold areas, a layer of snow helps insulate bulbs against low temperatures, but where possible carefully remove snow from the foliage of evergreen shrubs before it weighs down and disfigures branches.

▲ *Strongly constructed steps, recessed in a retaining wall, are attractive and give ready access to the border behind.*

▼ *An ornamental pond needs to be positioned in good light and where leaves cannot fall into the water in autumn.*

english flower gardens

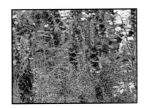

Few gardening styles are as relaxed and informal as an English country garden. Herbaceous borders are packed with plants that mostly die down to soil level in autumn, and develop fresh shoots and leaves in spring. Mixed borders are a medley of plants, including shrubs and bulbs.

▲ *The fleshy-rooted border perennial* agapanthus *creates a mass of large, umbrella-shaped flower heads mainly during mid- and late summer.*

Herbaceous borders

During the late 1800s the Irish garden writer William Robinson (1838–1935) published *The English Flower Garden*, in which he enthused about herbaceous perennials. He claimed that the English cottage had for many years been a repository for herbaceous plants. His writings came at a time when there was a general hunger for information about plants, and a popularization of gardening books and magazines. However, Gertrude Jekyll (1843–1932) is the best-known advocate of herbaceous plants. Her first book about these plants, *Wood and Garden*, appeared in 1899, followed by others that included ideas about single-colour borders. Pages 70–71 explain colour-themed borders, including pink and red, blue and mauve, yellow and gold, and white and silver plants.

Mixed borders

Few small gardens are able to devote more than a corner to a colour-themed border, and therefore borders inevitably tend to be a mixture of herbaceous perennials, bulbs, annuals, shrubs and trees producing a rich array of colours, sizes and shapes. Such borders create a good opportunity to have all the plants you like.

Hardy and half-hardy annuals are superb space fillers during the early years

of a mixed border. The half-hardy annuals are planted in gaps in early summer, as soon as all risk of frost has passed, while hardy annuals can be sown earlier. Remember to sow the seeds of hardy annuals thinly.

Bulbs provide extra colour and include lilies that delight in soil shaded and cooled by other plants. Clumps of snowdrops, crocuses and daffodils are very welcome early in the year and, although they leave a legacy of untidy leaves later on, they need little care and will appear year after year.

Hardy annual borders

If you have a passion for bright colours that can be changed each year then consider a hardy annual border. A few packets of seeds will produce glorious displays for months on end. However, avoid sowing seeds too early in the year; unless the soil is warm they will not germinate and they may even start to decay if conditions are too wet.

In windy areas, select moderately tall hardy annuals, and support them with twiggy sticks. A few annuals also have special appeal to children, particularly *Helianthus annuus* (sunflower), which has large, often 30cm/12in-wide, flowers and although some are 3m/10ft high, others are much lower and ideal in windy sites. They are easy to grow in a sunny position and look especially attractive growing against a white wall that highlights the yellow petals and their brown or purple centres.

▲ Use relatively low-growing and lax flowering plants to create bright edges to paths, especially where informality is desired.

◀ Floriferous herbaceous borders, with their relaxed and informal nature, are a traditional part of English gardens.

HARDY ANNUALS FOR ROCK GARDENS

Even in a small garden hardy annuals have a useful role, especially in rock gardens where they fill bare areas and add extra colour. Plants to choose from include:
❀ *Adonis annua* (pheasant's eye) – 25cm/10in high with deep crimson flowers with black centres.
❀ *Limnanthes douglasii* (poached egg plant) – 15cm/6in high with bright yellow-centred white flowers.

informal gardens

Informality in gardens appeals to many gardeners because it creates a more restful atmosphere than when plants are in straight, regimented lines and the borders have predictable shapes. Cottage gardens are the epitome of informality, where plants of many types grow together in a relaxed way.

Cottage gardens

To many gardeners, the key features of cottage gardens are secluded bowers, rustic trellises with scented climbers and beds patchworked with flowers, fruit and vegetables. There is even space for topiarized birds and animals trained in *Taxus* (yew) and *Ligustrum* (privet).

Armillary spheres, with their circular arrangement of rings that show the relative positions of celestial bodies are less formal than sundials, and add to the relaxed atmosphere.

To ensure an authentic cottage garden, you can also grow apple varieties with superb flavours. They include 'Ashmead Kernel', 'Egremont Russet', 'Ellison's Orange' and 'James Grieve'. Good pear varieties include 'Doyenne du Comice', 'Louise Bonne de Jersey' and 'Winter Nelis'. Runner beans on tripods in borders add height and create a background for other plants.

Wild gardens

Wild gardens are not a contradiction in terms but a way of bringing a hint of the wild landscape into a small, controlled environment. A light, overhead canopy of trees helps to create shade for plants from *Hyacinthoides* (bluebell) to azaleas. If you have inherited a garden with deeper shade you can partly alleviate the conditions by thinning branches, but in any case stick to shade-loving plants (see pages 44–45). Other good features to include are meandering rustic paths linking parts of the garden, and alpine 'meadows' with low-growing bulbous

◀ *Benches and other seats are essential in a garden, creating places from which it can be admired.*

plants in short grass, creating superb features in full sun, especially on a slope.

Wildflowers are also vital to attract a wide range of insects. Many seed companies sell special mixtures of wildflowers and they are best sown in the spring. Most will re-seed themselves during the following year and, although not all gardeners will wish to create such informal areas, they constitute an environmentally-friendly way of keeping a healthy garden.

Soothing sounds

Most gardens have colourful flowers and attractive foliage, but why not add comforting sounds as a new dimension? These can range from the rustling of leaves to the reassuring pitter-patter of water splashing and tumbling from fountains. Some plants are especially

known for their ability to create sound in even the slightest breeze. Grasses and bamboos rustle, and a gravel path with bamboos on either side is a joy throughout the year. Encourage birds and birdsong with a bird bath or feeding area away from cats. Remember to keep feeding the birds in winter but avoid whole peanuts, hard fat or too much bread during early spring when there may be young in the nests. At this time, fresh insects and worms are a better diet.

WIND CHIMES

Wind chimes suspended from trees and close to a house add a gentle and comforting sound to the garden, but do not put them somewhere they may cause irritation through being repeatedly knocked.

▲ *A meandering stream through a wildflower garden forms a captivating feature. A garden bench enables plants to be easily admired.*

▼ *Wildflower gardens are easily created and mixtures of wildflower seeds are available from seed companies. Always sow the seeds thinly.*

formal gardens

Regimented gardens appeal to many gardeners. They provide a neat appearance and a better opportunity than informal types to change arrangements of plants from spring to summer, as well as from one year to another. Small front gardens often have a formal design.

Carpet bedding

During the mid-1800s many low-growing, sub-tropical plants were introduced into gardens, and by the 1870s they were grown to form carpets of colour in borders. Most were planted in geometric patterns, but some formed monograms, especially in large estates.

The art of carpet bedding spread to botanical and municipal gardens, with each town competing to create the most

▲ *Formal gardens have a clinical nature that suits many small areas. Ponds, either round or square, create attractive features.*

original and attractive display. Some designs of carpet bedding were even used as advertisements, as commemorative notices and to depict the names of towns. Carpet bedding is still widely practised in popular coastal resorts.

Home gardeners pursue this type of gardening by growing half-hardy annuals in summer, and bulbs and biennials in spring and autumn.

Summer displays

Plant them in late spring or early summer, as soon as all risk of damage from frost has passed. The plants are raised from seeds sown in late winter or early spring in gentle warmth in greenhouses, and are later acclimatized to outdoor conditions. In addition to half-hardy annuals, plants with attractive foliage are also used and they range from *Bassia scoparia* 'Trichophylla' (Summer Cypress and still better known as *Kochia scoparia* 'Trichophylla') and *Euphorbia marginata* 'Summer Icicle' to *Abutilon pictum* 'Thompsonii'. They are often used to create height in a low display.

Traditional plants used in formal bedding displays include *Lobularia maritima*, still known as *Alyssum maritimum* (sweet alyssum), bushy forms of *Lobelia erinus* in colours including blue, white and red, and the many forms of *Tagetes* (marigold).

Spring displays

These usually involve a medley of biennials and spring-flowering bulbs, especially tulips. Biennials are sown in nursery beds in late spring or early summer, and are planted in borders in late summer or early autumn. Bulbs such as tulips are planted at the same time.

Spring displays can be a rich mix of colours, shapes and heights and include biennials such as *Bellis perennis* (common daisy), wallflowers, *Dianthus barbatus* (sweet William) and *Myosotis sylvatica* (forget-me-not). In late spring or early summer, after their display has finished, the plants are pulled up. The soil is then forked over, lightly firmed by shuffling over it, and planted with summer-flowering displays.

Knot gardens

Originally, the knot garden was an expression of the unchanging, endless nature of life. By the mid-1600s the knot garden had become a term for a flower garden surrounded and interwoven with paths. Today, it is more often associated with miniature hedges formed of *Buxus sempervirens* 'Suffruticosa' (dwarf box) and surrounding small flower beds. These intricate shapes are ideal used in the design of small gardens.

Formal ponds

Round ponds have a simple yet distinctive nature, especially when featured with a fountain. They need a formal setting, perhaps set in a wide lawn surrounded, at a distance, by a formal hedge of *Taxus baccata* (yew). Alternatively, construct wide paths around the pond and divide the surrounding area into quarters planted with summer-flowering bedding plants. In each of the beds use dot plants to create height.

FORMAL TOPIARY

Unlike topiary depicting animals and birds, which is ideal for cottage gardens, those shaped like cones, pyramids and squares are more suited to formal areas. These can be grouped, perhaps towards the end of a formal lawn, or sited throughout the garden to add interest.

▶ *Miniature hedges created by dwarf box are ideal for encircling a border, where they create formality without dominating the garden.*

paths for all gardens

Paths should not just be ribbon-like features providing quick access from one part of a garden to another – they should be attractive in their own right, with surfaces that harmonize with the rest of the garden. A wide range of construction materials are available for paths, and many are shown here.

Why have a path?

Paths are essential in many parts of a garden, especially an all-weather surface right around a house linking the garage, fuel store and sheds. But even these domestic demands do not mean that a path need be bland and unimaginative. Areas around cottages can have grey, ribbled-surfaced paving stones spaced 10cm/4in apart in a sea of shingle, or a natural stone path with spaces left for low plants. Modern houses demand a formality that is provided by a wide range of individual or mixed surfaces. Fortunately, a path running alongside a clothes line is now no longer a necessity thanks to the introduction of 'spinning' washing lines on a single pole.

Constraints and opportunities

The choice of materials for the construction of a path is influenced by the garden's topography and shape.

▶ *Crazy-paving paths are ideal for both flat and sloping gardens, as they can closely hug even the most twisting and undulating contours.*

Materials such as square or rectangular paving slabs are ideal for straight paths, whereas crazy paving is more adaptable and can be used for both straight and curved paths. Grass paths, with or without stepping stones running down their centres, can be curved or straight, while informal paths of thyme look particularly eye-catching when in flower.

A garden that is undulating or markedly sloped has a strong influence on the selection of materials. Crazy paving is perfectly suited to ground that slopes in several directions, whereas formal paths are best where the ground slopes in one direction. Shingle paths should be reserved for flat areas, as the shingle inevitably migrates slowly downhill.

Materials used to construct a path should be in proportion to its width. A path formed of a combination of small, rectangular and square paving slabs looks out of proportion if over 60cm/2ft wide. For a wider path use larger paving slabs. Conversely, narrow paths of crazy paving appear confusing, but look better when wider and irregularly shaped.

Medley paths

Paths can be formed of several different materials. Those for informal areas could include sections of tree trunks positioned as stepping stones in a sea of coarse gravel or concrete six-sided slabs with pebbles, while railway sleepers spaced 7.5–10cm/3–4in apart in cobbles or gravel also work well. In wild gardens, make shingle or grass paths edged with logs and in rural gardens where borders are wide, use sections of logs as stepping stones to give access to the entire area.

For formal gardens, the range of materials is much wider. Form patterns from different yet similarly textured and coloured paving slabs with gaps left for cobbles, but remember that this may make the path very uneven. Bricks and flexible pavers can also be laid in attractive patterns.

WINTER WARNING

Where plants are positioned in gaps between paving slabs, do not use salt to remove ice, or use a shovel or spade to scrape away snow. If possible, leave these winter hazards alone and let them melt naturally.

▲ *Informal paths formed of a well-drained but firm base covered with shredded bark and with a low, weaved edging are ideal for rustic gardens.*

▼ *Concrete pavers are ideal for forming straight paths in formal gardens. The pavers can be laid in straight lines as well as in complex patterns.*

walls and fences

Most gardens have a wall or fence to define boundaries, create privacy, deflect noise, and screen unpleasant views. The main constructional difference is that a wall needs strong foundations along its entire length, whereas a fence only requires support for the concrete or wooden posts.

◀ *Walls of all kinds, whether formal or informal, create secluded and cloistered spots with small, paved areas for garden furniture.*

Fence or wall?

Brick walls are much more expensive to construct than fences and, when 1.8m/6ft high, need to be 23cm/9in thick with strengthening piers every 1.8m/6ft. Even screen block walling (blocks 30cm/12in square and, 10cm/4in thick and with a latticework design) needs strong foundations and piers every 3m/10ft, as well as supports at the ends. Screen block walling can be attractively combined with a traditional brick wall or reconstituted stone bricks.

Fences range from white picket fencing to close-boarding, where the framework of the fence requires 10–15cm/4–6in wide pales (strips of wood) nailed to arris rails. Such fences are usually 1.2m/4ft to 1.8m/6ft high. Always select a fence to harmonize with the garden. For example, a picket fence is ideal for the front boundary of a cottage garden, whereas wattle fencing and chestnut paling are better suited for the back area. Panel fencing, with 1.8m/6ft long panels from 1.2m/4ft to 1.8m/6ft high, is popular and rather cheaper than close-boarding.

Post and chain fencing has a diminutive nature and is ideal for marking a boundary, but it will not keep people out. The chain is now usually made of strong plastic and needs no maintenance. Ranch-style fencing, where planks of wood 1.8–2.4m/6–8ft long and 15–20cm/6–8in wide are nailed to posts, has a modern, open feel. Gaps of about 10cm/4in are left between the planks, but to stop people looking through, nail planks on alternate sides of the supporting posts which are concreted into the ground. These fences can be 90cm/3ft to 1.8m/6ft high.

Cast-iron fencing is ideal for surrounding the front gardens of Victorian and Georgian town houses. This kind of fence is usually 90cm–1.8m/3–6ft high and painted black. The fences are very attractive and can be used as features on their own, or underplanted with a range of flowers.

Gates for all gardens

Walls and fences in front gardens are not complete without a complementary gate. White picket fences need rustic wooden gates while an old and weathered brick wall with an arch requires a wrought-iron gate with a round top.

The range of decorative patterns in wrought-iron gates is wide, and this is usually reflected in the cost. Wooden gates vary in style, and apart from the paling type there are overlapping board gates and those which feature diamond-slatted cladding.

▼ *Choose a fence that suits your garden. Wattle fencing panels, secured to stout posts, have an informal, rustic and cottage garden-like nature.*

THIEF-PROOF GATES

Wrought-iron gates are usually hung on peg hinges and can be quickly and easily stolen. To prevent this happening, secure the lower hinge to the post and with the peg upwards, hang the gate and secure the top hinge with the peg downwards. Now the gate cannot be lifted off. Wooden gates are usually more secure as the hinge is screwed to the gate and the supporting post.

steps for all gardens

Handsome flights of steps that harmonize with the rest of the garden become enduring features of interest. They must, of course, be functional, but there is no reason why they cannot also be attractive. Here is a range of steps that will enhance your garden, whatever its style or size.

Informal steps

Log steps are essential for wild gardens on slopes. Thick logs or old railway sleepers can be used to form the risers. They have a relaxing nature and can be enhanced by daffodils naturalized in the grass beside them. Avoid forming narrow ribbons of daffodils; instead plant them in wide groups, about one-third the width of the steps.

In small areas, consider naturalizing *Crocus chrysanthus* bulbs alongside a path. They flower in late winter and early spring and in a wide range of colours, including yellow, blue and bronze.

Consider planting trees on either side of narrow, informal steps set in a steep bank; this will create a light canopy of branches and leaves. Grass steps look good in informal and semi-formal gardens. Log steps with grass forming the treads are also informal, but they are not all-weather surfaces. For long flights of steps, a strimmer is essential for cutting the grass, whereas in small areas a pair of hedging shears is sufficient. Semi-formal grass steps use bricks at the edges of the treads, with grass behind them.

Formal steps

Large, wide flights of steps, especially those with wide areas at the top and base, create dominant features. Narrow steps in small gardens can also be attractive, especially when constructed with unusual materials. Bricks with a chamfered edge can be used as part of

▲ *A flight of garden steps, especially when constructed from attractive natural materials, creates a pleasing feature.*

the tread, with other bricks as the risers. Steps with a semi-circular design, and a full circle of bricks at the top, are very attractive and always capture attention. The inner parts of the treads can be formed using coloured gravels, bricks or grass. Semi-circular steps work well as a link between patio or terrace and grass lawn and between different levels of grass but do not attempt to form large flights of these steps; usually, three steps on a slight slope is sufficient.

RECYCLING SPIRAL STAIRCASES

Old spiral staircases are very decorative and can be used in basement gardens as a feature. They look good when cloaked in small-leaved *Hedera* (ivy), and supporting pots and small hanging baskets.

▼ *Wrought-iron spiral staircases create unusual features, either in basement gardens or, when shortened, as steps to a different level.*

shady patios

We owe the term 'patio' to the Spanish, who used it to describe an inner courtyard, surrounded by a dwelling and open to the sky. Patios were designed as an integral part of the house, which was usually single storey, to provide shade and shelter throughout the day.

Publicizing patios

The concept of patios spread from Spain to the southern states of the USA and then westwards to California, where they were ideally suited to the climate. Later, the term migrated to temperate regions in Europe, where it is often now used instead of the word terrace.

The L-shaped patio

Many houses have an L-shaped area outside a rear entrance that, with the addition of a fence, can become partly enclosed. Alternatively, use a free-standing trellis, erected about 45cm/18in from the boundary itself and with an L-shaped end, to create an even more cloistered area. To make an evergreen screen of foliage, erect a trellis and plant a large-leaved variegated ivy such as *Hedera colchica* 'Sulphur Heart' or *H. c.* 'Dentata Variegata'; both have variegated leaves. For summer foliage the

◀ *A secluded patio, shaded from strong sunlight, is an oasis of calm. Tables and benches are essential for outdoor living.*

herbaceous climber *Humulus lupulus* 'Aureus' creates a handsome screen of leaves. Where a flowering screen is desired, plant *Clematis montana*.

Surfacing patios

An attractive, well-drained surface is essential. It need not be consistent across the entire patio because you can leave spaces for shrubs and small trees. Other areas can be laid with cobbles, with large containers standing on top.

Paving slabs with raised patterns, brick-like slabs positioned together to create a pattern, and granite setts can all be used, but do avoid smooth, highly coloured and checkerboard surfaces.

Healing nature

Part of the enchantment of a patio is the opportunity to have cool, refreshing water splashing from a fountain into a central pond. Repetitive but irregular gentle sound has a therapeutic effect that helps to reduce stress. Also, an enclosed patio stops the scent of plants being blown away. *Helichrysum italicum* (curry plant) may well trigger memories of a visit to Asia, while the unforgettable bouquet of lilac may conjure up thoughts of a wedding bouquet. Many fragrances are more personal: a mistress of the world-famous novelist H. G. Wells claimed that his body emitted a honey-like fragrance. She could have recaptured this with the honey-scented bulbs *Crocus chrysanthus* or *Iris danfordiae*. Both plants can be grown beside paths, and in containers such as pots and window boxes.

ORNAMENTS ON PATIOS

Small statuary and ornamental pots are ideal for creating interest on patios. Additionally, large, barrel-like pots make superb homes for *Clematis macropetala*, with its tangled mass of stems and double blue flowers during late spring and early summer. It has the bonus of producing silky, fluffy seedheads.

▶ *An ornamental pond, with its calming and therapeutic qualities that help to reduce stress, is an ideal feature on patios.*

sunny terraces

Many houses and bungalows have a flat, all-weather surface at their rear which creates an outdoor leisure area. Correctly, a terrace is an open and usually paved area connecting a house with the garden. It usually has a balustrade or low wall, especially if raised above the general level of the garden.

Ancient heritage

Terraced landscapes with superb views were known in Thebes, Egypt, in about 1500 BC. This style of gardening progressed westwards to Italy, where terraces were created as status and power symbols, while giving views over the surrounding countryside. During the Middle Ages the viewing equivalent of a terrace was constructed on castle walls, while in 13th-century Spain the gardens on the hill slopes of the Alhambra had similar constructions. The English landscape designer Humphry Repton (1752–1818) was very keen on terracing, and in 18th-century England a variation known as the terrace walk became popular, with a surface of grass rather than paving. Such terraces were often long and especially sited to give views of the surrounding landscape. Grassed terraces were either straight or gently curved.

Versatile terraces

Most paved areas in temperate climates are terraces. They are usually adjacent to a house, open to the sky and, where possible, positioned to gain the maximum sun (unlike patios that are features of hot countries where shade is essential). The surface of terraces varies from natural stone paving, ideal for areas around cottages, to paving slabs that suit modern demands. Natural stone paving can be made even more informal by planting prostrate plants between the irregular-sized slabs. For formal terraces that dominate a garden, choose brightly coloured, smooth-surfaced slabs perhaps laid in a checkerboard fashion. For other formal areas where plants are cherished as much as they are on the patio use less dramatically coloured slabs, perhaps with a ribbled surface.

Occasionally, large terraces are constructed and include raised beds.

◄ *South-facing terraces bask in sun throughout summer. A garden pond, together with a fountain, creates a vibrant yet cool ambience.*

Plant them with shrubs and small trees to provide some shade. Tubs, ornamental stone sinks, pots, window-boxes and troughs are other worthwhile features.

Balustrades and walls

Traditional classical terraces inevitably had ornate, stone balustrades. Today, they can be superb when surrounding the edge of a terrace, giving it a hint of classicism. This style of feature is most appropriate for more formal architecture. Classical balustrades are totally unsuited to a modern brightly coloured area; a wall partly formed of screen-block walling with a concrete capping is much more appropriate. Also remember that safety is a priority along the edge of a terrace on a steep slope, especially when young children are present. A wall about 75cm/2½ft high is essential.

Wooden balustrades are seldom seen, although a form of ranch-style fencing about 75cm/2½ft high suits terraces formed of brightly-coloured, smooth-surfaced paving slabs. They can be painted white, and built even higher if privacy from prying eyes is needed.

▲ Where sunlight is strong throughout summer, attach canopies above patio windows. Ensure that they can be taken down in autumn.

▼ All-weather surfaces for terraces are vital. Ensure that they slightly slope away from the house so that torrential rain is not a problem.

courtyards

Courtyards have a long history and were used over 1,000 years ago in Islamic forts, palaces and religious buildings, where they formed shady areas out of direct sunlight and free from dust. They also became popular in temperate countries, particularly in towns and as parts of castles.

Shady and secluded

Today's courtyards in town gardens are usually small, secluded and protected from strong wind, although where gates are on the north side there is a risk of cold winter winds searing the foliage of evergreen plants. Courtyards inevitably have shady areas but this need not be a problem as many plants, including ferns, grow in shade and moist soil (see pages 44–45). You can also grow almost anything from small trees to bulbs in containers in the sun.

Seclusion and shade appeal to many gardeners, especially in towns where privacy is hard to find. Shade from strong sun during the day is welcome but in the late evening the gloom can often make the area too dark to use. One solution is to have spotlights and concealed lighting fitted by a competent electrician.

Basement flats sometimes have cloistered areas. These can be treated as

courtyards, with the addition of plants in containers. Usually they have stone steps connecting them with ground level and these can be made more attractive by planting trailing plants such as variegated forms of *Vinca minor* (lesser periwinkle), beside them. Plant it towards the top, so that it can trail freely downwards. The prostrate *Lysimachia nummularia* (creeping Jenny or moneywort) will also brighten the edges of steps, and grows well in

partial shade. For extra colour choose the form 'Aurea' with yellow leaves, but it does demand slightly more light.

Flooring a courtyard

A wide variety of paving materials is available. Large, aged, well-worn flagstones are ideal, but they can be difficult to obtain and are usually expensive. Alternatives are brick pavers, granite sets and reconstituted flagstones.

▶ *Courtyards have a secluded and often partly shaded nature. Use plants in pots and tubs and select those that thrive in shaded areas.*

Cobbles are another possibility but they are difficult to walk on.

Furniture and gates for courtyards

Wrought-iron or aluminium furniture with an aged, ornate nature suits a cloistered, shady courtyard. Besides harmonizing with the walls, non-ferrous metal furniture does not deteriorate, although it is usually necessary in spring to scrub off lichen and moss. Wooden furniture, such as benches with integral tables and seats, are always much in demand. In late autumn stand each leg on a brick, and cover the entire table with a plastic sheet securely tied down to protect it from the winter weather. Collapsible, slatted furniture has the advantage that it can be taken indoors and stored. Finally, ornate, wrought-iron gates are ideal for entrances to courtyard gardens; they are not as dominant as wooden doors and allow the outside world to be seen at a glance.

▲ *Courtyards are not complete without furniture; wrought-iron is ideal for these small areas as it takes up little space and can often be folded for storage.*

EARLY MOTELS

In the Near and Far East caravanserais, or caravansary, have been known for many centuries. These were caravan hostels for merchants and travellers built around a large courtyard.

pergolas, arches and trellises

Pergola-type constructions were known in warm countries from the earliest times, and in Egypt were probably used to support vines and create shade. The Italians took up the idea and came up with the term 'pergola', meaning an arbour, bower or walk of bowers mainly covered with vines.

Pergolas for all places

Pergolas can be informal, formal or even oriental. Those constructed from rustic poles, often astride paths, are ideal for giving support to leafy climbers such as *Vitis vinifera* 'Ciotat' (parsley vine). The cut-leaf nature of the leaves has a more relaxed, informal nature than the ordinary vine. If an informal flowering climber is desired, choose *Lonicera periclymenum* 'Belgica' (early Dutch honeysuckle) or *L. p.* 'Serotina' (late Dutch honeysuckle). *Lonicera japonica* (Japanese honeysuckle) also has a free-flowing show of flowers.

Formal pergolas formed of planed timber, with square-cut uprights and cross beams, create ideal supports for wisteria. Although wisteria can be grown against a house wall, it is better where the large bunches of flowers can hang freely. Also, being a vigorous climber it soon drains the border soil around a house of any moisture which can be detrimental to both the house and other plants growing alongside.

An oriental look can be given to formal pergolas by cutting the underside edges and ends of the cross beams at a sloping angle. Lean-to pergolas are another variation and often assume the nature of an arbour. Proprietary brackets are available for securing the cross beams to a wall, with wooden uprights on the other side.

◀ *Most pergolas are straight and straddle paths, but an alternative use is to enclose a rounded area perhaps devoted to growing bush roses.*

Arches

At their simplest, arches are just inverted hoops over a path covered in climbers from roses to the leafy herbaceous climber *Humulus lupulus* 'Aureus'. However, the ingenuity of gardeners has ensured arches of all shapes and sizes, including four-way arches at the junctions of paths.

Use arches to create height and focal points, as well as to grow climbers. Increasingly, metal arches are used to grow roses both over paths and as features on lawns where, when covered in leafy plants, they assume the role of an arbour. Indeed, metal and wooden arches against a wall or fence will create an attractive and romantic arbour.

Trellises

Traditionally, trellises were secured to walls, but increasingly they are used as free-standing features to provide privacy and to create smaller areas, each with a different nature. They are also ideal for screening dustbins.

Rose enthusiasts welcome free-standing trellises as an opportunity to grow more climbers. At the end of a broad lawn erect a line of trellises, with other shorter ones at right-angles to them. This produces features resembling stalls for horses. Pillar roses, where both climbing and rambling-type roses are grown up rustic poles or tripods of sawn timber, can be integrated into the display to create a variety of shapes.

▲ *Plants that reveal their flowers at eye-level create exciting gardens, with flowers and scent where they can be readily appreciated.*

▼ *Trellises attached to walls create ideal homes for climbing roses, as well as other climbers that require a supporting framework.*

arbours and tunnels

Arbours and tunnels come in all shapes and sizes, and are mainly admired for their romantic, cloistered and leafy nature. Arbours are usually covered in flowering and leafy climbers, while tunnels often have flowering or fruiting trees trained over a wooden or metal structure.

▲ *Laburnum trained over metal arches is awash with long, pendulous clusters of yellow flowers during late spring and early summer.*

Arbours for all gardens

There are arbours for all gardens, and many are ideal for small areas, where they fit into corners or alongside walls. Increasingly, arbour units are sold either fully constructed or 'in the flat', and are ready to erect, complete with a bench-like seat. Informal types are made of rustic poles, and formal ones of sawn timber. Additionally, some are made of wrought iron and have a delicate, aged nature that suits roses and less vigorous climbers, such as *Clematis orientalis* (Oriental clematis), *C. tangutica* and *C. macropetala*.

More noticeable are arbours in the centre of a garden, perhaps forming an eye-catching central feature. They need a firm, paved base to provide an area for seats and chairs, and perhaps a small, low table. Sometimes, arbours are constructed on a base slightly above the surrounding area; this often suits more formal gardens. Informal arbours, perhaps with a floor created by natural stone paving, look better at ground level. Crazy paving has a semi-formal nature that also suits ground-level arbours.

Tunnels

Tunnels are ideal for channelling people from one part of a garden to another, and if a sundial, ornamental well or seat is positioned at the far end it creates an attractive focal point. Tunnels often have a decorative quality, especially when clothed in laburnum or climbing roses. Additionally, apples and pears can be planted to clothe a series of metal arch-like hoops. Brambles were traditionally used to create fruiting tunnels. Nut walks were also popular, but these did not rely on large hoops of wire for support. Rather, the branches were pruned so that they formed a kind of tunnel over a rustic path.

In short gardens, do not make a tunnel long as it highlights the garden's lack of length. Because of their symmetrical nature, tunnels are often constructed centrally. Where a garden is divided by a cross-wise free-standing trellis, bisect it with a tunnel. This helps to divide the garden and to lead the eye into a further part of it. Feature a herb garden at the end of a fruit tunnel. Alternatively, position a sundial or seat as a focal point, with a circular gravel path around it with beds for the herbs.

▲ A wrought-iron framed gazebo has an open nature that is ideal for creating homes for climbing roses and other lax, flowering climbers.

▲ Cloistered corners, heavily canopied with leafy and flowering climbers, create secluded and romantic areas in gardens.

◀ A small gazebo creates a superb feature, especially when positioned on a firm surface and nestling among shrubs and border plants.

37

porches and entrances

Porches prevent rain saturating people on arrival at a door. Large and ornate porches are often built around a front door, while less decorative and more functional types are at the rear. Additionally, rustic or formal arches can be secured to walls around doors.

Brightening porches

A bare area around a front door creates the impression of blandness and neglect, but when a porch-like structure is fitted it brightens the house and garden, especially when covered in leafy plants or flowers. Where a permanent brick-built structure is not possible, use arches purchased for DIY assembly or complete. Fit rustic arches around cottage doors, and formal types for more modern houses. Where extra weather protection is desired, secure an unobtrusive piece of wood to the top, either to form a flat roof or one with a pitch. Eventually, this will be covered by the climber. Always secure the arch to the wall and ensure that the four posts are concreted into the ground, so that they remain firm. The weight of climbers can be deceptively heavy, and winter winds may loosen weak fixtures.

The insides of large porches can be decorated with hanging baskets with drip trays in their base, and a bright show of tender plants. In summer they can range from *Campanula isophylla* (star of Bethlehem) to *Chlorophytum comosum* 'Variegatum' (spider plant) and tradescantias. And in summer, the outside can be festooned with hanging baskets

◀ *Climbing plants enrich the outsides of entrances, creating a warm and friendly ambience in the garden and the house.*

suspended from brackets. Take care not to put them where the basket will be knocked against, or where water will drip on to plants below. At ground level, hardy plants in containers can be left outside all year. They include narrow conifers, clipped box and half-standard bay trees in tubs.

Apart from brightening a porch, both inside and out, the wall that surrounds it can be made colourful throughout the year. Secure pieces of narrow trellis to the wall on either side of the porch. Position each piece about 23cm/9in from the outer edge of the porch and plant variegated evergreens or flowering plants to cover them.

Brightening gates and entrances

Front gardens bordered by a hedge such as a common privet or yew can be given a fresh identity by training branches to form an arch over a path. The training takes several years and is best performed on a tall hedge. Where paths are long, consider a metal or wooden arch over the path, positioned about two-thirds along it. Climbing roses clustering over metal arches are suitable for both formal and informal areas, whereas those constructed of rustic poles are strictly for cottage gardens and are ideal for supporting honeysuckle or jasmine.

Where there is not room for an arch, one or two pillar roses on either side of a path introduces height to a garden. Alternatively, plant a weeping standard rose on either side of a path, but about 1m/3½ft from its edge.

▲ Small porches form a useful and attractive shelter from wind and rain. Linking them with a boundary fence creates a unified feature.

▼ Wrought–iron gates and rustic entrances are especially attractive when roses or honeysuckle are trained over an arch.

39

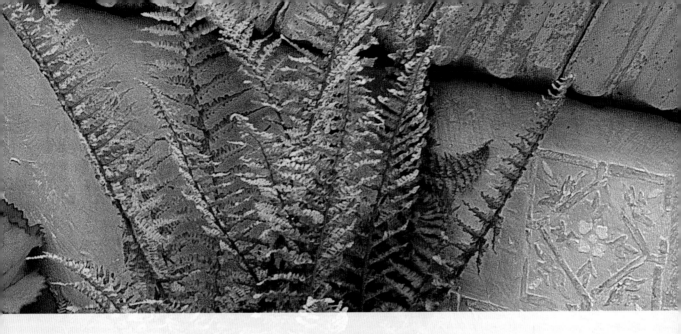

creating your garden

Selecting features for a garden is one of the most exciting parts of gardening and these range from water gardens and colourful borders to secluded and scented corners that will delight you with a range of fragrances throughout the year. Bush and climbing roses are also possibilities, as well as paths formed of herbs. And whether you have a heavily shaded garden, or one that continually basks in sun, there are plenty of plants that will surprise you with their resilience.

gardening in full sun

Many plants, including hardy annuals, herbaceous perennials and shrubs, grow well in strong sunlight. Unfortunately, hot sunshine inevitably means dry soil, but this is not an insurmountable problem. A surprisingly large number of plants grow in these conditions.

Living with dry, hot soils

Full sun invariably means dry, impoverished soil unless provisions are made to improve it. These include digging in plenty of well-decayed garden compost or manure to increase the soil's ability to retain moisture. Additionally, thoroughly watering the soil and then adding a 7.5cm/3in-thick mulch aids moisture retention and keeps the soil cool.

Mulches of pea shingle or stone chippings in rock gardens and scree beds will keep the soil cool and moist.

Hardy annuals for full sun

A few hardy annuals grow well in sun or partial shade, but some are especially at home in full sun. Adding well-decayed garden compost or manure to the soil in winter, followed by regular watering throughout summer, are vital aids to success, particularly in hot, dry places. Sun-loving hardy annuals include

▶ Achillea *(yarrow) flourishes in strong sunlight and contrasts well with hollyhock, a hardy perennial usually grown as a biennial.*

- *Agrostemma githago* 'Milas' (corn-cockle)
- *Argemone polyanthemus* (prickly poppy)
- *Asperula azurea* (woodruff)
- *Calendula officinalis* (pot marigold)
- *Carthamus tinctorius* (safflower)
- *Centaurea cyanus* (cornflower)
- *Eschscholzia californica* (Californian poppy)
- *Godetia amoena*
- *Gypsophila elegans* (baby's breath)
- *Iberis amara* (annual candytuft)
- *Lavatera trimestris* (annual mallow)
- *Limnanthes douglasii* (poached egg flower)
- *Malope trifida*
- *Nicandra physaloides* (shoo fly plant)
- *Nigella damascena* (love-in-a-mist)
- *Phacelia dubia* (Californian bluebell)
- *Scabiosa atropurpurea* (pincushion flower)
- *Xeranthemum annuum*

Herbaceous plants for dry, sunny borders

Because herbaceous perennials produce fresh leaves, stems and flowers each year, they need to grow rapidly and without restriction from spring to autumn. Many Mediterranean plants survive a combination of full sun and dry soil, especially those with silver leaves. Excellent herbaceous perennials that survive well in full sun and dry soil include:

- *Achillea millefolium* (yarrow)
- *Alstroemeria ligtu* 'Hybrids' (Peruvian lily)
- *Anaphalis triplinervis*
- *Asphodeline lutea*
- *Baptisia australis* (false indigo)
- *Buphthalmum salicifolium* (willow-leaf ox-eye)
- *Catananche caerulea* (cupid's dart)
- *Centaurea macrocephala*
- *Echinops ritro* (globe thistle)
- *Eryngium*
- *Gypsophila paniculata* (baby's breath)
- *Heliopsis scabra* (orange sunflower)
- *Limonium latifolium* (sea lavender)
- *Nepeta × faassenii* (catmint)
- *Solidago* (goldenrod)
- *Stachys byzantina* (lamb's tongue)

Shrubs for dry, sunny borders

Again, thorough soil preparation is essential before planting. First-rate shrubs for full sun and dry soil include:

- *Artemisia abrotanum* (lad's love/southernwood)
- *Artemisia absinthium* (common wormwood)

▲ *Achillea is an ideal herbaceous perennial for growing in a dry, sunny border. Its flowers are ideal for cutting and displaying indoors.*

- *Brachyglottis* 'Sunshine' (better known as *Senecio* 'Sunshine')
- *Buddleia davidii* (butterfly bush)
- *Caryopteris × clandonensis* (bluebeard)
- *Ceratostigma willmottianum* (Chinese plumbago)

CONTAINER GARDENING

Container gardening is popular in hot, sunny countries and a wide range of sun-loving plants can be grown in pots, tubs and window boxes. And if pots and tubs are put in groups, perhaps to one side of a patio, they can be more easily watered. This grouping also helps keep the containers cooler than they would be if positioned separately. If pots and tubs at the back of a group cannot be easily reached when being watered, tie a stiff 1.2m/4ft-long bamboo cane to the end length of hose pipe so that you can hold it out.

- *Choisya ternata* (Mexican orange blossom)
- *Cistus* (rock rose)
- *Cytisus × praecox* 'Warminster' (Warminster broom)
- *Genista aetnensis* (Mt. Etna broom)
- *Hebe speciosa* (shrubby veronica)
- *Helichrysum italicum* (curry plant)
- *Lavandula angustifolia* (lavender)
- *Lavatera* 'Rosea' (tree mallow)
- *Kolkwitzia amabilis* (Beauty bush)
- *Romneya coulteri* (tree poppy)
- *Rosmarinus officinalis* (rosemary)
- *Salvia officinalis* (common sage) – several coloured leaf forms
- *Spartium junceum* (Spanish broom)
- *Ulex europaeus* 'Plenus' (double-flowered gorse).

gardening in shade

Most gardens have shady areas, perhaps created by a house, large tree, fence or hedge. Such places can be a problem, but they also create opportunities to grow a wider range of plants. In fact, once established, many plants grow in shade, in both dry and moist soil.

Getting plants established

Plants in dry, shady areas are more difficult to establish than those in moisture-retentive soil. Dig dry areas thoroughly and mix in plenty of well-decayed garden compost or manure.

▲ *Many leafy plants thrive in shade. In this moist area,* Fatsia japonica *forms a perfect corner feature in a border and alongside a path.*

If the soil is impoverished, perhaps under trees or around the bases of shrubs, it will need a dusting of fertilizer. However, take care not to boost the growth of existing plants. Instead, add bonemeal to the planting hole, and a couple of times during the first year fork in a general fertilizer around the stem. Whatever happens, regularly water plants until they are established. Also lay a 7.5cm/3in-thick mulch around plants every spring. In moist, shady areas ensure that the soil is adequately drained by adding sharp sand. The danger in these areas is that the plant roots may rot and die.

Plants for dry shade

Many highly attractive shrubs are sufficiently resilient to survive these conditions, and they include *Mahonia aquifolium* (Oregon grape), which has leathery, glossy green leaves and fragrant, rich yellow flowers in spring. *Ruscus aculeatus* (butcher's broom) is another tough shrub. Symphoricarpos (snowberry) and osmanthus are other suitable shrubs. Good herbaceous

perennials include *Anaphalis margaritacea*, with grey-green leaves and pearly white flowers in late summer. Its near relative *Anaphalis triplinervis* also grows in dry shade. For a taller and more dominant display, plant *Crambe cordifolia* (colewort), which grows 1.5–1.8m/5–6ft high. It has branching stems with white flowers in early summer. Epimediums grow about 30cm/12in high and are ideal for covering the soil with colourful leaves and flowers. *Persicaria affinis* (still better known as *Polygonum affine*) also makes good ground cover.

Plants for moist shade

Several shrubs flourish in moist soil and shade, including camellias, *Elaeagnus angustifolia, Gaultheria shallon, Gaultheria procumbens* and *Fatsia japonica*, with its distinctively large, glossy green leaves. Herbaceous perennials include *Aruncus dioicus* (goat's beard), *Brunnera macrophylla, Cimicifuga racemosa* (bugbane), hostas, *Lysimachia nummularia* (creeping Jenny), *Pulmonaria angustifolia* (lungwort) and *Rodgersia pinnata*.

Climbers and shrubs for a shady wall

It is inevitable that one side of a wall will be in shade. Fortunately, there are climbers that grow well, even on the north and less congenial side of a wall. *Garrya elliptica* is an evergreen wall shrub that grows on both sunny and shady sides of walls, but it flowers best on the brighter side. *Hydrangea anomala petiolaris* (Japanese climbing hydrangea) is a vigorous climber that does well on a north or north-east wall, and its creamy white flowers appear during early summer. *Jasminum nudiflorum* (winter jasmine) also grows well on an almost sunless, north-facing wall, and produces yellow flowers during winter. Several pyracanthas with attractive berries grow against both sunny and shady walls.

Shade-loving ferns

Most ferns grow in shade and damp soil although some will thrive in dry areas that are fully shaded. Visit a specialist nursery and you will find a wide range of plants that are easy to grow and a very useful addition to the shaded border. Ferns for moisture-retentive soil include *Asplenium scolopendrium* (hart's-tongue fern) (also known as *Phyllitis scolopendrium* or *Scolopendrium vulgare*), *Matteuccia struthiopteris* (shuttle-cock fern); *Onoclea sensibilis* (sensitive fern) and *Osmunda regalis* (royal fern). Ferns suitable for inhabiting dry soil, as well as modestly moist soil, include the widely grown *Dryopteris filix-mas* (male fern), *Adiantum pedatum* (Northern maidenhair fern), *Athyrium filix-femina* (lady fern) and *Polypodium vulgare* (common polypody).

GROUND-COVER PLANTS IN SHADE

There are many suitable plants, but first take the opportunity to improve the soil (see previous page). Plants include:

- *Ajuga reptans* (bugle)
- *Alchemilla mollis* (lady's mantle)
- *Bergenia* (elephant's ears)
- *Epimedium* (barrenwort)
- *Hedera* (ivy)
- *Hypericum calycinum*
- *Lamium maculatum* (dead nettle)
- *Pachysandra terminalis*
- *Tellima grandiflora*
- *Tiarella cordifolia*
- *Vinca* (periwinkle)

▼ *Many ferns thrive in shade and moist soil, although some do well in dry soil. Here is a superb example of a fern with* Fatsia japonica.

creating lawns from seed

In temperate regions there are two main ways to create lawns, by sowing seed or laying turves. There are other ways, and in warm countries dibbling tufts of grass about 7.5cm/3in apart is successful, while in tropical countries spreading a mud plaster of chopped grass, water and soil is successful.

Preparing the site

Whether creating a lawn from seed or by laying turves, preparation of the soil is the same. First, check that the ground is well drained and, if necessary, install drains. In winter, dig the soil, removing perennial weeds. A few weeks before sowing seeds, rake the area level or with a slight slope. Firm the soil by systematically shuffling sideways over the area, so that it is uniformly firm. Do not use a roller. Rake the soil to create a fine tilth.

Sowing lawn seed

About a week before sowing lawn seed (usually in late spring, or from late summer to early autumn), evenly scatter a general fertilizer over the area at 50g per sq m/1½oz per sq yd. Use a metal rake to lightly mix it into the surface. Wait for a day when the surface soil is dry, and use string to section the area into 1m/3½ft-wide strips. Then, use a couple of 1.2m/4ft-long bamboo canes to form a 1m/3½ft square at one end of the strip.

  Into this area sow lawn seed at the rate of 50g per sq m/1½oz per sq yd. Sowing less than this amount results in a thin, sparse lawn, while too much produces masses of tightly bunched seedlings susceptible to disease.

  Next, move one of the canes to form a further square and sow with more seed, continuing in this way until the whole area has been covered. Then, while standing on a plank of wood, lightly and evenly rake the seed into the surface. It is important that you do not walk on sown areas because the soil gets depressed and seed may stick to your shoes. If the weather forecast indicates a dry period, lightly but thoroughly water the soil. Also provide protection from hungry birds. Stretch black cotton about 15cm/6in above the surface and 20cm/6in apart, but ensure that birds cannot be harmed. Alternatively, large sheets of black polythene laid on the sown surface give protection and retain moisture. However, they must be removed immediately germination occurs.

▶ *Lawns create a natural foil that shows off plants to perfection. Additionally, grass paths are superb for connecting parts of a garden.*

ADVANTAGES OF SOWING SEEDS

⊛ Cheaper than laying turves.
⊛ Lighter work than laying turves.
⊛ Easier to create intricately shaped areas.
⊛ There is lawn seed for almost every part of the garden, from sunny sites to shady areas, and from play areas to ornamental lawns.

DISADVANTAGES OF SOWING SEEDS

⊛ It takes from 3–4 months before a lawn can be used.
⊛ Cats often disturb the sown surface, and dogs and toddlers may tread on it.
⊛ Perennial weeds can be a problem if the area has not been thoroughly prepared.

HINTS AND TIPS

Always buy a little more seed than you will need. Often, small bare areas occur and it is useful to have the same type and batch of seed to re-sow them.

lawns from seed

1 Level the soil and remove any large stones. Work in a general fertilizer at 50g/sq m or 1½ oz/sq yd using a garden rake or metal-tined lawn rake.

2 Stretch two garden lines across the area to be sown, either a metre or yard apart. Then, place two 1.2m/4ft-long garden canes to form a square yard or metre.

3 Evenly scatter seed into each square at the rate of 50g per sq m or 1½ oz per sq yd. Ensure that each part of the square is sown, and not just the centre.

4 When the square has been sown, move one of the canes to form another square. Then, repeat the sowing process until the row is complete. Use a garden or lawn rake to lightly work the seed into the surface.

creating lawns from turves

Lawns made of turves are thought to be instant features but be warned, you will have to wait at least four weeks before they are established and can be used. Soil preparation is exactly the same as when creating lawns from seed (pages 46–47).

Laying turves

Turves can be laid from spring to autumn, although early autumn is the most popular period because the soil is warm and usually moist. After thoroughly preparing the soil use a metal rake to level the surface and, about one week before laying turves, scatter a general fertilizer at 70g per sq m/2oz per sq yd. Lightly rake it into the surface.

Mark out the area to be laid and stretch a garden line down one edge. As an insurance against dry weather and damage to the edges, make the area about 7.5cm/3in wider than required; should the edges become dry the lawn will not be spoiled because it can be cut back to the desired size.

Start laying the lawn by positioning a row of turves along the garden line, closely abutting their ends. Then, place a 20cm/8in-wide and 2.4–3m/8–10ft-long plank of wood on top of the turves. Stand on this plank (moving it as necessary) to lay a further row of turves. Stagger the joints. Again, move the plank and lay a further row, continuing until the whole area is covered.

Always ensure that each turf is in close contact with the soil by using a 'firmer' made from a thick, 45cm/18in-square piece of wood attached at its centre to a vertical handle, usually a thick,

1.5m/5ft-long pole. Inevitably, gaps occur between the turves, both at their ends and sides. Trickle a mixture of equal parts of sieved soil and peat substitute into them. Then thoroughly water the surface.

Types of turf

There are two main types of turf used to make garden lawns. The first is meadow turf cut 90cm/3ft long, 30cm/12in wide and 36mm/1½in thick; but expect variations. It comes from pasture and is usually the cheapest way to buy turves. Cultivated turf is the other type and is sometimes known as seeded turf. It is grown especially for sale, costs more than meadow turf and is sold in rolls, but before buying do check the exact size because it can vary.

ADVANTAGES OF LAYING TURVES

⚙ A usable surface is usually created about four weeks after laying.
⚙ Eliminates problems with birds, cats and dogs.
⚙ Ideal for families with young children.
⚙ Turves can be laid from spring to autumn, but not when the soil is dry. If it becomes dry, regular watering is essential.

DISADVANTAGES OF LAYING TURVES

⚙ More expensive than sowing seeds.
⚙ Much heavier work than sowing seeds.
⚙ Turves have to be laid within 24 hours of delivery. If left rolled up, the grass becomes yellow and the edges begin to dry. If laying is delayed, be prepared to unroll the turves and water them.

HINTS AND TIPS

Always buy a few more turves that you need. This is important where the sides of a lawn are curved. Also note that because turves are laid in a staggered pattern there is always some wastage at the ends.

laying turves

1 Thoroughly prepare the soil and rake in a general fertilizer. Stretch a garden line along one side of the planned lawn and lay a turf alongside it. Lay further turves, with their ends butted against each other.

2 Put a wide, strong plank on top of the laid turf and stand on it to lay a further line, closely abutting the first row and with the end joints staggered. Never stand directly on the turf as it causes indentations.

3 Use a firmer, made from a thick piece of wood 45cm/18in square, with a vertical pole 1.5m/5ft long, fixed at its centre as a handle. Stand on the plank and firm the turf so that it is in close contact with the soil.

4 Trickle a mixture of sieved soil and a peat substitute into the joints and use a broom to work it into the cracks. When the lawn is complete, use a sprinkler to gently but thoroughly soak the entire area.

▲ A well-manicured lawn creates a sense of space as well as highlighting plants and other garden features.

chamomile lawns, thyme paths

These create colourful and unusual features that can be fitted into most gardens, whatever their size. Chamomile lawns have a long history and were popular with the Elizabethans, who played bowls on their scented surface. Paths formed of scented thyme also create another exciting feature.

Chamomile lawns

They are grown with *Chamaemelum nobile*, earlier and widely known as *Anthemis nobilis*, a prostrate, mat-forming herbaceous perennial with finely dissected leaves that release a fruity scent when bruised and walked on. The non-flowering variety 'Treneague' has a banana-like scent.

Weeds can be a problem in new chamomile lawns and thorough preparation is necesary. Dig the area 30cm/12in deep in winter and remove all perennial weeds. Leave for 12 months, regularly pulling or digging up weeds as they appear. In the second winter, dig the soil again and plant in the spring.

Planting a chamomile lawn

Rake the area level and systematically shuffle sideways over the surface to firm it evenly. Then, rake again to remove foot-prints. If dry, thoroughly water the soil and wait until the surface is lightly dry and crumbly

before planting. You can plant the lawn in late spring or early summer. Space the plants 15–20cm/6–8in apart in staggered rows, and use a trowel to make holes that do not constrict the roots of each plant. Check that the crown of each plant is slightly below the surface, then firm the soil and lightly but thoroughly water the entire area. When the plants start to form a lawn, use sharp hedging shears to trim them.

Thyme paths

Use *Thymus serpyllum* (English or wild thyme) to form a colourful, scented path. It is evergreen and carpet-forming, with grey-green leaves that have a rich fragrance, and bears white to pink to red flowers through much of the summer. When established, this thyme has a 45–60cm/18–24in spread, but for rapid cover set the plants closer together.

Creating a thyme path

During winter, mark the path's width and thoroughly dig the area to remove perennial weeds. Leave the surface rough so that the weather will break down the surface to a fine tilth. In spring, rake the soil and place stepping stones on the surface (check with your family to ensure their spacings suit everyone). Then, set them into the ground so that the surface of each stone is about 12mm/½in above the soil's surface. To ensure a quick covering, set individual plants 23–30cm/9–12in apart. Firm the soil around them and thoroughly water the entire area. Until established, regularly water the path, especially at its edges where the soil becomes dry.

▲ *Chamomile lawns, formed of finely dissected mid-green leaves with a fruity and chamomile-like fragrance, always attract attention.*

▶ *Thyme paths become decorative ribbons of colour throughout summer and are ideal for linking one part of a garden with another.*

SCENTED SEATS

These create unusual features in small gardens and are basically bench-like areas, about 45cm/18in high, 1.2–1.8m/4–6ft long and 50–60cm/20–24in deep, planted with chamomile or thyme. Because the area is raised the soil tends to become dry, especially if the weather is hot and sunny, in which case regular watering is essential. A variation on this kind of seat is to intersperse the plants with small paving slabs. As well as providing sitting positions the slabs help keep the soil cool and moist.

water gardens

Water introduces tranquillity and vitality to a garden. Established garden ponds, perhaps nestling in an open, sunny corner of a garden, create a restful ambience, especially when covered with waterlilies, and with dragonflies hovering over the surface.

Water features for all gardens

Water features do not necessarily involve a pond, and these alternatives are ideal when there are young children. Such features usually involve a fountain splashing over pebbles or water, in a shallow trough that is recirculated by a pump. It is usually positioned on a patio.

Traditional ponds with waterlilies, marginal plants and fish can be constructed to any desired shape or size. The water's surface can be level with surrounding ground or raised by about 45cm/18in. Additionally, ponds at ground level with an informal outline can be merged with a bog garden or wildlife pond. Several decades ago, ponds were nearly always square or rectangular, and made of concrete. Their construction was labour intensive and, without reinforcement, soon cracked. Bowl-shaped ponds with gently sloping sides are now a popular choice.

Today, ponds are mainly formed using a flexible liner (frequently called a pool liner) or come as a rigid liner (known as a pre-formed pond or a

▲ *Garden ponds introduce tranquillity and peace into a garden. The range of plants is wide, from waterlilies to fragrant marginal plants.*

SELECTING FOUNTAINS

❀ The spray should not fall on waterlilies or marginal plants.
❀ The height of the spray should not be more than half the pond's width.
❀ In windy areas, use fountains that produce large droplets of water.
❀ Do not allow water droplets to disturb floating plants.

moulded shell). Flexible liners are used to line holes dug to the desired shape and depth. Their longevity depends on the type of material; those made of polyethylene (polythene) are low cost and have a relatively short life, especially when exposed to sunlight. Butyl sheeting is the best, but also the most expensive material, and lasts for over 20 years. The liners must be laid on an underlay to prevent the water's pressure from puncturing them on sharp stones. Ready-made rigid liners are sunk into a hole; the lifespan again depends on the material, which ranges from plastic, the cheapest but with the shortest life, to glassfibre shells with a life expectancy of 20 years or more.

Choosing waterlilies

These need careful selection to ensure vigorous varieties do not dominate and overcrowd small ponds. Waterlilies are usually put into four classifications – dwarf, small, medium and vigorous. Dwarf types suit ponds with a depth of 10–25cm/4–10in deep; small lilies need a 15–45cm/6–18in depth; the medium lilies need 30–60cm/1–2ft depth, and the vigorous type need a water depth of 45–90cm/1½–3ft.

When planting a waterlily, put it in a plastic mesh container with compost and cover with a 2.5cm/1in-thick layer of clean pea shingle. Soak the compost and place the container in the pond. Using bricks as a stand for the container, position it so that the plant's leaves float on the surface. As the plant grows, progressively remove the bricks.

Mini-ponds on patios

Even a patio or terrace in the smallest garden can have a water feature. Stout wooden tubs are ideal summer homes for miniature waterlilies and other aquatic plants. Unfortunately, the small volume of water usually makes it necessary to either empty the tub in winter or to move it to a greenhouse or conservatory. First-rate miniature waterlilies include:

▲ *A raised pond creates a distinctive feature on a patio. Ensure that the materials used in its construction harmonize with other features.*

Nymphaea 'Aurora' – pinkish-yellow, then orange and later red.

Nymphaea 'Graziella' – orange, with orange-red stamens.

Nymphaea tetragona – white, with yellow stamens.

Marginal aquatics include:

Carex elata 'Aurea' – narrow, golden leaves.

Scirpus tabernaemontanii 'Zebrinus' – quill-like stems banded green and white.

FLEXIBLE LINER

Mark out the approximate position of the pond with string, then a garden hose to indicate the shape and size. Dig out the area, forming a shelf about 30cm/12in below the surface for the marginal plants. Check that the top and the shelf are level. Then use a spade to remove a strip about 25cm/10in wide and 5–7.5cm/2–3in deep from around the pool for the edging stones. Remove any stones from the surface and line the base with soft sand.

Position the liner and temporarily weight its edges with paving. Fill the pond using a hose pipe and adjusting the weights so that the liner takes the shape of the hole. Trim the liner so that 15–20cm/6–8in can be folded back and edging stones cemented into position.

creating a rock garden

Rock gardens make ideal features in small gardens, especially as a large number of small plants can be grown in them. Also consider a rock garden on a gentle slope and free-standing mounds created from well-drained soil, with stones added in stratified rows to produce attractive features.

Rock gardens

If you are fortunate enough to have a garden with a slope towards the south or west, a rock garden is easily created with pieces of natural stone such as limestone or sandstone positioned to resemble stratified rows. For a rock garden with an area of about 4.5sq m/15sq yds you will need between 1–2 tons/tonnes of stone.

The range of plants for rock gardens is wide and includes alpines and small herbaceous perennials, dwarf bulbs, and miniature and slow-growing conifers. Additionally, dwarf shrubs such as *Cotoneaster linearifolius* grow about 30cm/12in high and 50cm/20in wide and give a permanent structure. There are many other shrubs including thyme,

the glorious yellow-flowered *Hypericum olympica*, and *Zauschneria californica* (Californian fuchsia) with red, tubular, fuchsia-like flowers during late summer and early autumn.

Free-standing rock gardens

These have natural stone in stratified layers, like a rock garden on a slope. They often provide more space for plants than a 'slope' type because it is possible to plant the front and two sides. Since the front is usually small, do not dominate it with large, shrub-like plants but use miniature, columnar and slow-growing conifers to create the impression of height. These include *Juniperus communis* 'Compressa' (45cm/18in high after 10 years) and

STAR PLANTS

Aubrieta deltoidea	*Sedum acre*
Aurina saxatilis	*Saponaria ocymoides*

◀ *Rock gardens that are harmonised with a gently flowering stream are immediately more interesting than when on their own.*

Juniperus scopulorum 'Skyrocket' (1.8m/6ft high after 10 years). Where interest is needed at the rock garden's base, giving the impression of extra width, plant *Juniperus squamata* 'Blue Star' (38cm/15in high and 60cm/24in wide after 10 years) or *Juniperus × pfitzeriana* 'Gold Sovereign' (50cm/20in high and 75cm/30in wide after 10 years).

Dry-stone walls

These look superb when their sides are covered by colourful flowers. Several rock garden plants can do this but perhaps none better than *Aurinia saxatilis*, better known as *Alyssum saxatile*. On a dry-stone wall it spreads 30–45cm/12–18in wide, and trails golden-yellow flowers more than 60cm/24in). There are several attractive varieties. *Aubrieta deltoidea* is an evergreen perennial that bears cross-shaped flowers in shades of rose-lilac to purple in spring and early summer.

In addition to plants that clothe the sides, grow others at the top so that their tumbling foliage cloaks the wall's sharp outline. Such plants include *Saponaria ocymoides*, with pale pink flowers through most of the summer that trail to about 60cm/2ft, and *Sedum acre* 'Aureum',

which has bright yellow flowers and spreads to about 60cm/2ft. Raised beds are similar to dry-stone walls, but with the wall encircling a 45–90cm/1½–3ft high bed up to 1.5m/5ft wide.

Scree beds

Scree beds are often placed around rock gardens. However, in very small gardens they are a superb feature on their own. Suitable plants to grow in scree range from miniature and slow-growing conifers to dwarf bulbs and perennials such as aethionema, erodium, *Phlox douglasii* and silene.

▲ *Scree beds are ideal for small gardens and can be added to an existing rock garden or constructed as features on their own.*

MAKING A SCREE BED

A scree bed is very easy to construct. Mark out an area at the base of a rock garden, so that it widens out like a mushroom. Dig the area 38cm/15in deep and fill with 15cm/6in of clean rubble. Over this spread a 5cm/2in layer of course sand. Mix a compost of one part top-soil, one of moist peat

substitute and three of sharp grit and spread a 15cm/6in layer over the entire area. Position rocks as if they were a small outcrop from the main rock garden. Plant the alpines in the compost. Spread a 2.5cm/1in layer of shingle over the surface to reduce water loss.

bush and shrub roses

The range of large-flowered bush roses (hybrid teas) and cluster-flowered bush roses (floribundas) is wide, and each year many more are introduced. Additionally, there are many species roses with a dramatic and subtle range of colours. There are also the more recent New English Roses.

Using roses

It was earlier thought that the only way to grow bush roses was in formal beds flanked by paths or lawns. Today, they are used in many other situations – prostrate types to cover the soil, patio roses alongside patios, species roses in shrub borders, and weeping standards in beds and lawns. Also, small rose bushes can be planted in rock gardens or used in window-boxes. These include 'Baby Masquerade' (yellow to pink and red), 'Cinderella' (white, tinged pink), 'Darling Flame' (orange-red, with yellow anthers), 'Green Diamond' (lime-green) and 'Pour Toi' (creamy white).

Weeping standards are well known for their beautiful, cascading outlines. They are created by nurserymen budding a variety on a rootstock about 130cm/51in high. When mature, the head is 1.5–1.8m/5–6ft high, with stems cascading from the top. Mainly rambler varieties are used and include 'Albéric Barbier' (cream), 'Crimson Showers' (red), 'François Juranville' (salmon-pink) and 'Goldfinch' (yellow, fading to white).

Companion planting bush roses

The pleasure given by bush roses can be increased by planting them in attractive groups. Plant the buttercup-yellow floribunda 'Allgold' in front of *Clematis* 'Countess of Lovelace', a large-flowered variety that will flourish sprawling over a fence or garden wall. The latter flowers through summer into autumn (double-flowered forms bloom during summer, and single types in late summer and autumn). Its deep lavender flowers create a handsome feature with those of the rose. Underplant white-flowered bush roses with the evergreen perennial *Tiarella cordifolia* (foam flower), which has a low mound of maple-like leaves and creamy white flowers in late spring and early summer.

▲ *Rosa gallica officinalis, (apothecary's rose or red rose of Lancaster) bears large, loosely-formed, semi-double, rose-crimson flowers.*

The popular Floribunda 'Queen Elizabeth' has cyclamen-pink flowers that look superb highlighted against yew. Plant the large-flowered yellow 'Grandpa Dickson' against the dark purple leaves of the deciduous shrub *Berberis thunbergii* 'Atropurpurea'. And, for additional colour, plant the half-hardy annual *Nicotiana* 'Lime Green' in front of them.

Companion planting shrub roses

The range of shrub roses is wide and historical. They range from Albas to Moss roses, and form attractive combinations with other plants. The Alba 'Königin von Danemark' has deep pink flowers that look superb when seen against the silvery leaved, weeping tree *Pyrus salicifolia* 'Pendula'. Another splendid collaboration is the modern shrub rose

'Nevada' with creamy white flowers, and blue delphiniums and campanulas. The 'New' English Rose 'Constance Spry' has pink flowers best highlighted by a surrounding of silver-leaved plants.

PATIO ROSES

This is a relatively new group of roses, coming between miniature roses and small floribundas. They are sometimes called dwarf cluster-flowered bush roses and are ideal alongside a patio. Even when you are sitting down they do not obstruct the view. Most are between 45cm/1½ft and 60cm/2ft high, and include 'Anna Ford' (vivid orange-red), 'Claire Rayner' (striped orange and yellow), 'Mandarin' (deep pink with orange-yellow centre), 'Robin Redbreast' (red, with a pale centre) and 'Top Marks' (bright, vivid orange-vermilion).

▲ *Roses create distinctive backgrounds for low border plants and often enrich the air around garden benches with rich fragrances.*

▼ *Many shrub roses have an informal and relaxed nature and can be allowed to cascade and spread slightly over paths and lawn edges.*

climbing and rambler roses

Climbers and ramblers create dramatic features in gardens and can be made even more spectacular when the colour complements its background. A white wall produces an ideal backcloth for roses with yellow or scarlet flowers, whereas a grey stone wall is better for those with pink or red flowers.

Climber or rambler?

Both climbers and ramblers produce attractive flowers, but each has a distinctive nature. Climbers have a more permanent framework than ramblers and their flowers, when compared with ramblers, are larger and borne singly or in small clusters. Ramblers have long, flexible stems that sometimes grow up to 3–3.6m/10–12ft in one season and bear flowers in large trusses, usually only once a year.

Covering trees

Old, perhaps slightly unsightly trees can be transformed by training climbers to scramble up through their branches. Plant them several feet to one side of the trunk, and replace the soil with a mixture of top-soil and well-rotted garden compost or manure. Firm the compost, plant the rose, water the soil and use a stout cane to guide the stems to the tree trunk.

Suitable varieties range in vigour, and can be selected to suit the tree that needs brightening. Roses to consider include 'Blush Rambler' (2.7m/9ft, rambler, pale pink), 'Emily Gray' (4.5m/15ft, rambler,

butter-yellow); 'Mme Grégoire Staechelin' (climber, 6m/20ft, rosy carmine-pink), 'Paul's Himalayan Musk' (rambler, 9m/30ft, blush-pink), 'Sympathie' (climber, 4.5m/15ft, blood-red) and 'Wedding Day' (rambler, 7.5m/25ft, creamy white to blush).

Pillar roses

Ideal in small gardens, all you need is a rustic pole 2.4–3m/8–10ft high or a tripod formed of rough-cut timber. In quite a small area, several pillars can be

◀ *Pergolas and free-standing trellis provide support for many roses. They can be positioned alongside paths and edges of lawns.*

GROUND-COVER ROSES

Ground-smothering roses do not actually form a weed-suppressing blanket of stems, leaves and flowers, but they do provide a low mass of colour. Good choices include 'Max Graf' (pink), 'Nozomi' (pearly-pink to white), 'Partridge' (white), 'Rosy Cushion' (pink) and 'Snow Carpet' (white). The County Series includes 'Avon' (pearly white), 'Essex' (rich reddish-pink), 'Hertfordshire' (carmine-pink) and 'Wiltshire' (pink).

inexpensively constructed. Climbers with moderate vigour are ideal for clothing such structures and include 'Bantry Bay' (semi-double, deep pink), 'Compassion' (salmon-pink, tinted apricot-orange), 'Handel' (creamy blue, edged pink), 'Pink Perpétue' (bright rose-pink) and 'Reine Victoria' (shell-pink).

Climbers for cold walls

This situation is not ideal for roses, but a few sturdy ramblers and climbers survive such conditions and produce acceptable displays. Hardy and vigorous varieties to consider include 'Albéric Barbier'

(rambler, cream), 'Félicité et Perpétue' (rambler, white), 'Morning Jewel' (climber, bright pink), 'New Dawn' (climber, pink blush) and 'Zéphirine Drouhin' (climber, deep pink).

Companion planting climbers and ramblers

In the same way that bush roses can be planted in attractive arrangements with other plants, so can climbers and ramblers. For example, the rambler 'Bobbie James', which is often grown over pergolas and clambering up trees, has large clusters of semi-double, creamy

white flowers that create an attractive feature with the lavender-blue flowers of *Nepeta × faassenii* (catmint), a bushy perennial growing about 45cm/18in high. It flowers throughout summer. Another good combination is the modern climber 'New Dawn', with semi-double, blush-pink flowers with the vigorous hybrid *Clematis* 'Perle d'Azure' with light pink flowers. It flowers from early to late summer.

▼ *Rose 'Helen Knight', a distinctive climber, creates a mass of small, buttercup-yellow flowers in late spring and early summer.*

cottage gardens

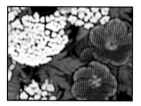

Few gardening styles have such a relaxed and informal nature as a cottage garden. It is rich in nostalgia, and packed with flowers, fruits, vegetables and herbs. Such informality can easily be created in small gardens, with arbours and trellises providing secluded areas.

Screening plants

Few climbers compare with the scrambling *Clematis vitalba* (old man's beard), widely seen in hedgerows. It is usually remembered for its glistening, silky seed heads in autumn that often continue into winter. Elizabethans praised it for covering hedges, but in a small cottage garden it is too vigorous and there are other clematis with more attractive and delicate flowers. They include *Clematis macropetala*, *C. flammula* (fragrant virgin's bower) and *C. orientalis*. *C. montana* is also attractive but often too large for small areas. Honeysuckle is also an excellent cottage garden climber, best given rustic supports. And before being grown for food, runner beans were used as screening plants; try them clambering up a 1.8m/6ft-high tripod.

Cordon and espalier apples also create screens and, where possible, plant some of the older varieties with superb flavours and textures. Try the cooker 'Annie Elizabeth', and for eating 'Ashmead's Kernel', 'Charles Ross', 'Egremont Russet' and 'James Grieve' to bring back the flavour of 'real' apples.

Flower borders

Aim for a medley of shrubs, trees, herbaceous perennials, bulbs and annuals planted or sown in attractive groups, each plant complementing its neighbours. From spring to autumn memorable plant associations can be created.

❀ Spring – tulips offer a wide range of colours; for a mixture of yellow, orange-red and blue try a deep-blue forget-me-not and a combination of orange-red and yellow tulips. If you prefer a medley of blue, scarlet and gold flowers, plant pale blue forget-me-nots and the scarlet and gold single early tulip 'Keizerskroon'. Alternatively, for a white and blue display, plant a carpet of the biennial *Bellis perennis* (common daisy) with blue Parrot-type tulips. These arrangements are ideal for beds and under windows. For a larger spring display in a prominent border plant the yellow-flowered deciduous shrub *Forsythia* 'Lynwood' with small groups of red-flowered Kaufmanniana tulips.

▲ *The large, dominantly coloured flowers of* **Papaver orientale** *(Oriental poppy) create a dramatic display during early summer.*

STAR PLANTS

Clematis montana	*Hydrangea macrophylla*
Geranium endressii	*Sedum* 'Autumn Joy'

❀ Summer – *Lilium candidum* (Madonna lily) has pure white flowers, and is an ideal companion for foxgloves, which have tall stems bearing bell-shaped flowers in a colour range from purple, to pink to red. For a climber and herbaceous association, plant a combination of the scrambling *Clematis flammula* (fragrant virgin's bower), with small, sweetly-scented flowers, and *Aconitum napellus* (monkshood) with its deep blue, helmet-shaped flowers.

Roses are also superb in summer displays. 'Buff Beauty' bears warm, apricot-yellow flowers that form a pleasing partnership with the lavender-blue *Nepeta* × *faassenii* (catmint) and *Papaver orientale* 'Perry's White' (Oriental poppy). Another good combination involves the Damask rose 'Mme Hardy', with white flowers, and pink varieties of *Geranium endressii*. The Bourbon rose 'Mme Isaac Pereire' is bushy and shrubby, with crimson flowers that harmonize with tulips, lilies, paeonies and lilacs.

❀ Autumn – for a large display, plant blue varieties of the hardy, deciduous dome-shaped shrub *Hydrangea macrophylla* in front of the evergreen shrubby *Eucryphia* × *nymansensis*, with cream flowers. Another duo perfect for autumn display is the evergreen border plant *Sedum* 'Autumn Joy' and the bulbous *Colchicum* 'Waterlily'. The *Sedum* is well known for its richly coloured autumn flowers, eventually becoming orange-brown as the season progresses.

▲ A combination of tulips and fragrant forget-me-nots (myosotis) never fails to capture attention in spring and early summer.

▼ Border geraniums produce magnificent displays throughout summer. There are many varieties and colours.

scented gardens

Scented flowers and aromatic leaves can enrich the air with many different fragrances. The range of scents is amazingly wide, and even in temperate regions there is a choice of over 100 fragrances. They include scents from chocolate and pineapple to banana and lemon.

Creating a scent-friendly garden

The perfect site for a fragrant garden is one that is sheltered from strong wind that disperses scent, is free from frosts that limit the growing period of tender plants, and has a gentle slope towards the sun to create a warm ambience that encourages stronger fragrance. Clearly, few gardens have all these qualities but many can be created by planting hedges, erecting free-standing trellises and choosing frost-free areas to introduce tender plants.

Flower borders

Many herbaceous perennials have delicious scents, none more so than the short-lived, hardy herbaceous perennial *Hesperis matronalis* (Damask violet). The white, purple or mauve flowers appear in early and mid-summer and drench borders with a sweet fragrance, especially during evenings. *Saponaria officinalis* (common soapwort) also has a sweet scent, with single, pink, salver-shaped flowers during mid- and late summer. Perhaps better known is *Phlox paniculata*, with exceptionally sweet flowers from mid- to late summer; there are many varieties, in colours from white to pink and red.

◀ *This pairing of English lavender (Lavandula angustifolia) and rue (Ruta graveolens) brings scent and colour to small gardens.*

Many annuals quickly create summer colour and rich fragrances, and a mix of *Matthiola bicornis* (night-scented stock), with dull lilac flowers during mid- and late summer, and *Malcolmia maritima* (Virginian stock) is sure to enrich your garden. Sow them in friable soil underneath windows, and in successive sowings from spring to mid-summer.

Once associated with the Empress Josephine Bonaparte, *Reseda odorata* (mignonette) is a cottage-garden hardy annual with clusters of small, white and yellow richly scented flowers throughout summer. It can also be grown in window boxes and pots on balconies. It is said

AROMATIC-LEAVED SHRUBS

Caryopteris x clandonensis – pungent
Choisya ternata (Mexican orange blossom) – orange
Lavandula angustifolia (lavender) – lavender
Rosmarinus officinalis (rosemary) – rosemary
Ruta graveolens (rue) – pungent and acrid

that success and good fortune will attend a lover who rolls in a bed of mignonette!

Several diminutive bulbs are also superb at creating colour and scent for rock gardens and the edges of paths. Both *Galanthus nivalis* (common snowdrop) and *Iris reticulata* (netted iris) have violet-scented flowers during late winter and early spring.

Trees and shrubs

Many trees and shrubs are known to have sweet scents, but some have an unexpected fragrance. *Prunus padus* 'Watereri' (bird cherry) has a deciduous and spreading nature, with drooping tassels of white flowers, almond-scented in early summer. *Prunus × yedoensis* (Yoshina cherry) also has this scent. For a cowslip scent try the deciduous shrub *Corylopsis pauciflora*, with pale primrose yellow flowers in mid and late spring. And for a feast of exotic curry fragrance try *Helichrysum italicum* (curry plant).

If honey-like fragrances are more appealing, plant the informal *Ulex europaeus* 'Flore Pleno' (double-flowered gorse). The deciduous philadelphus shrubs have flowers with a sweet orange-blossom fragrance that will pervade the garden in mid-summer. The slightly tender *Cytisus battandieri* (Morrocan broom) bears pineapple-scented, golden-yellow flowers needing a warm, south-facing wall and the deciduous tree *Malus coronaria* 'Charlottae' has violet-scented, semi-double, shell-pink flowers.

STAR PLANTS

Galanthus nivalis
Helichrysum italicum
Hesperis matronalis
Phlox paniculata
Ulex europaeus 'Flore Pleno'

▼ *Few scented cottage garden plants are as attractive as* Hesperis matronalis *(sweet rocket), with its rich sweetness during summer evenings.*

ground-cover plants

Plants that smother soil with foliage prevent the growth of weeds and are welcome in any garden. The choice is wide and includes herbaceous perennials, shrubs and a few climbers such as large-leaved ivies like Hedera colchica 'Sulphur Heart'.

Border perennials

Most are herbaceous but some do retain their foliage through winter. Most prefer full sun or light shade, but others will grow out of the sun.

❀ Sun or shade – although some plants can grow in either light or shade, do not expect the same display in both. Most plants when given plenty of light and moisture will flower better than those in shade with little moisture. The range of plants you need includes *Alchemilla mollis* (lady's mantle) with lime-green, hairy leaves and yellow-green, star-shaped flowers. Bergenias, with their large, elephant-like leaves, also flower in spring. Epimediums are daintier and cover the ground with heart-shaped leaves that assume attractive tints in autumn and through much of winter. *Geranium grandiflorum* is herbaceous, with a spreading nature and blue-purple flowers in early and mid-summer. And *Hemerocallis* (day lily) forms large clumps, with arching, strap-like leaves and lily-like flowers. Avoid heavy shade because this reduces its ability to flower.

Persicaria affinis (knotweed) forms mats of lance-shaped leaves and poker-like flower-heads during mid- and late summer. *Saxifraga umbrosa* (London pride) has a more diminutive nature, with rosettes of leaves that carpet the soil and masses of pink, star-shaped flowers during late spring and early summer. *Lamium galeobdolon montanum* 'Florentinum' (better known as *Lamium galeobdolon* 'Variegatum') is vigorous and spreading, with silver-flushed evergreen leaves that display bronze tints in winter, and avoid dark shady places.

◀ *Smothering the ground with plants looks attractive as well as making gardening easier by eliminating the need to pull up weeds.*

Lysimachia nummularia (creeping Jenny) has sprawling stems of rounded leaves and bright yellow, cup-shaped flowers during early and mid-summer.

⚘ Partial shade – the popular *Ajuga reptans* 'Atropurpurea' (bugle) has purple leaves, while *Brunnera macrophylla* has heart-shaped foliage and sprays of blue flowers in late spring and early summer; it dislikes dry soil. The range of hostas is wide and, with their often large leaves, they soon cloak the soil. *Pulmonaria angustifolia* (with the evocative name blue cowslip) has lance-shaped leaves and funnel-shaped, blue flowers in spring. *Pulmonaria saccharata* has leaves spotted silver-white. *Symphytum grandiflorum* spreads rapidly, with tubular, white flowers during spring, while *Tiarella cordifolia* (foam flower) is less dominant, with maple-like, light green leaves.

⚘ Full sun – in strong sun, plant *Nepeta* × *faassenii* (catmint). It covers the soil with grey-green leaves and lavender-blue flowers from spring to autumn. The woolly leaved *Stachys byzantina* (lamb's tongue) never fails to attract attention.

Ground-covering shrubs

Many evergreen shrubs with a sprawling or bushy nature are ideal for covering soil with leaves and, sometimes, flowers.

STAR PLANTS

Alchemilla mollis
Hedera colchica 'Sulphur Heart'
Stachys byzantina

Hypericum calycinum (rose of Sharon) is a robust, ground-smothering plant that establishes itself quickly and even covers large banks. Throughout summer it bears golden-yellow flowers. Vincas also smother soil, but are best kept out of mixed lower beds because they are invasive. However, variegated forms are less invasive than all-green types. *Calluna* (heather) and *Erica* (heath) soon cover the ground with attractive leaves and flowers. Like *Gaultheria procumbens* (partridge berry), heathers and ericas need an acid soil. There are many others, including *Pachysandra terminalis*, with deep green leaves.

▼ *Where a large, flat area is planted with ground-covering plants, position large stepping stones to make access and maintenance easier.*

ornamental hedges

Creating hedges is more than just forming a boundary or screen. They can be gloriously rich in scents, have colourful berries, colour contrasts within the same hedge, and harmonize or constrast with nearby plants. Even the ubiquitous privet can be attractive.

Hedge duos

To create an unusual privet hedge plant a row alternating two plants of *Ligustrum ovalifolium* 'Aureum' to one of *L. ovalifolium*. This ratio will help prevent the more vigorous all-green type smothering the yellow form while maintaining the decorative nature. Clip the hedge regularly to keep it in shape. Another formal hedge, with a particularly slow-growing nature, can be created from variegated holly and yew, both evergreens. Plant them alternately, each about 1.2m/4ft wide.

Fragrant hedges

There is an amazing range of fragrances, from both leaves and flowers, and encompassing apple and raspberry. There are even several conifers that are used to create hedges emitting unusual fragrances when their foliage is bruised.

For an apple-like scent plant *Thuja occidentalis* 'Smaragd'; its dark-green foliage creates a dramatic backdrop for other plants. If a lemon-like fragrance delights you, choose *Cupressus macrocarpa* 'Lutea'. It has soft yellow foliage that, with age, becomes light green. The pineapple-scented *Thuja plicata* (western red cedar) has scale-like, shiny, rich green foliage with white marks underneath. It is best reserved for a large boundary hedge. A fusion of resin and parsley is produced by *Chamaecyparis lawsoniana* 'Allumii' with soft blue-grey foliage, and *Chamaecyparis lawsoniana* 'Fletcheri' with feathery, blue-green leaves.

◀ *The evergreen shrub* Berberis darwinii *(Darwin's berberis) has masses of rich orange flowers in spring, followed by blue berries.*

Roses used as hedges offer more unusual scents, none better than 'Zephirine Drouhin' with raspberry-scented, vivid pink flowers, and 'Penelope' has musk-scented, pale pink, semi-double flowers that fade slightly as they age. Several roses used for hedging have a sweet fragrance, including *Rosa rugosa* 'Roseraie de l'Hay' with crimson-purple flowers, 'Felicia' with salmon-pink flowers and 'Prosperity' in creamy white. Two evergreen shrubs with memorable scents include *Lavandula angustifolia* 'Hidcote', with deep purple flowers 5cm/2in long and silver-green leaves. *Rosmarinus officinalis* (Rosemary) also creates a superb informal hedge.

Harmonies and contrasts

Colour-themed herbaceous borders were traditionally backed by hedges that harmonized or contrasted with them. For example, the dark green leaves of yew highlight white, orange, blue and green borders, while golden-variegated holly harmonizes with golden borders. Tamarisk (*tamarix*) was frequently used as a backcloth for a grey border. The deciduous *Fagus sylvatica* (beech), with young leaves that darken from bright green in spring to mid-green in summer, creates an ideal backdrop for herbaceous plants. In autumn the hedge has the bonus of leaves that gain yellow and russet tints, competing for attention with end of season flowers and seed heads. Even in winter, when its leaves fall, it continues to create a backdrop.

▼ *Many roses can be used to form floriferous screens. They introduce a relaxed and cottage-garden nature.*

BERRIED DELIGHTS

Several shrubs used to create informal hedges also have attractive berries. These include:

Berberis darwinii – evergreen, holly-like leaves and clusters of rich orange flowers in spring, followed by blue berries.

Berberis × *stenophylla* – evergreen, with golden-yellow flowers in spring, followed by a peppering of globular, purple berries with a white bloom.

Hippophae rhamnoides (sea buckthorn) – deciduous, with thick clusters of orange berries during autumn and early winter.

Rosa rugosa 'Roseraie de l'Hay' – deciduous, with crimson-purple flowers, followed by large, round, orange-red hips in early autumn.

using plants in
small gardens

The range of plants, from flowers to vegetables and fruits, is wide and many have a reserved nature that makes them ideal for growing in small gardens. Several rootstocks for apples and pears have a dwarf nature and therefore are ideal for small areas, while growing peaches and nectarines against walls saves space. But it is flowers that create the most impact in a garden and borders and beds rich in a kaleidoscope of colour are irresistible.

pink and red garden schemes

Red is a dramatic, fiery dominant colour in gardens, especially when used en masse in full sun, while pink is a desaturated red with a warmer feel. The perceived nature of red changes through the day; in strong light it is bright but as evening approaches it assumes darker shades until almost black.

Flower borders

There is a wide choice of red and pink flowers for herbaceous borders and flowering bedding displays that will carry the colour scheme through from early spring into autumn. In herbaceous borders the plants range from tuberous-rooted alstroemerias, through the red and pink forms of the late-flowering *Aster novi-belgii* and *Aster novae-angliae* (both Michaelmas daisies), to the dramatic red flowers of *Schizostylis coccinea* 'Major', which is aptly known as the crimson flag. Many dahlias, from the smaller ball varieties to giant decoratives with flowers 25cm/10in wide, have excellent red flowers and will provide strong accents of colour in late summer.

Spring flowering displays, using bulbs and biennials, planted in late summer or early autumn, add plenty of colour. For a red and blue display, perhaps at the top of a dry-stone wall, plant a blue-flowered form of *Aubrieta deltoidea* with 'Madame Lefeber' tulips, below. Summer displays, mainly of seed-raised plants, also add red and pink flowers, but none so arresting as *Begonia × semperflorens* (wax begonia) and *Salvia splendens* (scarlet sage).

◄ *Pink and red are romantic colours that create a 'warm' ambience in a border. Pink flowers remain visible in the diminishing light of evening.*

Trees and shrubs

They produce both massed displays and distinctive individual flowers. The spring-flowering deciduous azaleas, often in demure shades of red and pink, are a sure sign that gardens are bursting into life. A wild garden, with a high and light canopy of leaves, provides the right setting: many have the bonus of richly-coloured leaves in the autumn.

Other shrubs with pink or red flowers include the magnificent *Hibiscus syriacus* (shrubby mallow) and *Kolkwitzia amabilis*, aptly known as the beauty bush for its pink, foxglove-like flowers with yellow throats. More dramatic and distinctive are the flowers of the deciduous, spring and early summer flowering *Magnolia liliiflora* 'Nigra'. Its flowers are upright, 7.5cm/3in long and deep reddish-purple. Offering a totally different style, the deciduous shrub *Leycesteria formosa* (pheasant's berry or granny's curls) has pendulous flowers formed of small, white flowers surrounded by highly conspicuous dark-claret bracts. It has the bonus of purplish-red berries in the autumn, which are attractive to pheasants.

Climbers and wall shrubs

The excellent range includes climbing and rambling roses, clematis and the rhizomatous-rooted *Tropaeolum speciosum* (flame creeper) which dies down to soil level in the autumn. From mid-summer to autumn the creeper produces scarlet, trumpet-like flowers on long stems and loves to clamber through shrubs. Several large-flowered clematis have red or pink flowers and include the popular 'Nelly Moser'; each pale mauve-pink petal has a soft crimson stripe. 'Ville de Lyon' is bright carmine-red and 'Ernest Markham' is vivid magenta with a velvet sheen.

▲ *Many quite different plants create attractive combinations. Here a rose and a variety of slow-growing conifers form a pleasing group.*

▼ *Low beds, perhaps at the edge of a rock garden and mainly planted with pink and red plants, create a feature that radiates warmth.*

Key to planting

1 *Myosotis* (forget-me-not)

2 *Primula* 'Wanda'

3 *Candelabra primulas*

4 *Anemone × fulgens*

5 *Magnolia liliiflora*

6 Rhododendrons

7 Azaleas

8 *Aubrieta deltoidea* (aubrieta)

blue and purple borders

Blue is a calm colour and used in gardens will provide an atmosphere of tranquillity. Blue colour schemes are thought to reduce blood pressure and slow up respiration and pulse rates. Enhance the colour by adding patches of dull white and pale-lemon flowers, but not strong yellows.

Flower borders

Blue-flowered herbaceous borders usually come to life at the start of summer, when suddenly they abound in colour. Perhaps no herbaceous perennial is more noticeable than *Delphinium elatum*. The large-flowered or elatum types have

▲ *Blue flowers create a contemplative and restful garden, while purple is more dramatic and looks best used in smaller groups.*

stiffly erect stems tightly packed with florets during early and mid-summer, while the Belladonna forms are smaller, gracefully branched, and superb in cottage gardens. Within each type there is a wide range of colours.

Several perennial asters are blue, including *Aster amellus* (Italian starwort) with large, daisy-like flowers that reveal yellow centres. 'King George' is especially attractive, with soft blue-violet flowers. *Aster × frikartii* 'Mönch' is slightly less dramatic, with lavender-blue flowers. Again, the flowers have golden centres. Other blue-flowered herbaceous plants include *Echinacea purpurea* (purple coneflower) with purple-crimson, daisy-like flowers and distinctive large central cones, *Physostegia virginiana* (obedience plant) with spires of pink-mauve flowers, and *Tradescantia × andersoniana* 'Isis' (Spiderwort) which bears three-petalled, purple-blue flowers.

Several spring-flowering bulbs have blue flowers and include *Hyacinthus orientalis* (common hyacinth) and *Muscari armeniacum* (grape hyacinth), which is an

ideal companion for polyanthus. *Myosotis alpestris* (forget-me-not) is a hardy perennial invariably grown as a biennial for its small and fragrant, azure-blue flowers borne in large clusters. There are many varieties and most will happily increase by self-seeding.

Summer-flowering bedding plants include blue-flowered forms of *Ageratum houstonianum*, such as 'Blue Danube' with masses of lavender-blue flowers, and *Lobelia erinus* with varieties such as 'Blue Moon' and 'Cambridge Blue'. There are also trailing forms, ideal for planting in window-boxes and hanging baskets.

Key to planting

① *Aster amellus*

② *Delphiniums*

③ *Corylus maxima 'Purpurea'*
(Purple-leaved filbert)

④ *Cotinus coggygria 'Notcutt's
Variety'*

⑤ *Hydrangea macrophylla*
(common hydrangea)

⑥ *Echinacea purpurea*
(purple cone flower)

⑦ *Physostegia virginiana*
(obedience plant)

⑧ *Ageratum houstonianum*
(flossflower)

Trees and shrubs

There are few blue-flowered trees
and shrubs but they do create
magnificient displays. *Cercis
siliquastrum* (Judas tree) has clusters of
rich, rose-purple flowers on bare
branches in early summer. Markedly
different is *Ceanothus × delileanus* 'Gloire
de Versailles', with long spires of fragrant,
powder-blue flowers from mid-summer
to early autumn. And most popular of all
are the blue-flowered forms of *Hydrangea
macrophylla* (common hydrangea).

Several shrubs and trees have richly
coloured leaves, including *Corylus
maxima* 'Purpurea' (purple-leaved filbert),
Cotinus coggygria 'Notcutt's Variety' with
deep-purple leaves, and *Berberis thunbergii*
'Atropurpurea' which bears small, rich
purple-red leaves.

Climbers and wall shrubs

These provide superb displays and none
more so than California lilacs. Look for
Ceanothus impressus with clusters of deep
blue flowers in spring, and *C. thrysiflorus*

▲ *This partly cloistered water garden creates an
oasis of peace and tranquillity.*

repens with light-blue flowers. Clematis
need support and few surpass *Clematis
macropetala*, with double, light- and dark-
blue flowers in late spring and early
summer. Other blue-flowering climbers
include *Solanum crispum* (Chilean potato
tree), *Wisteria floribunda* 'Macrobotrys'
and *Abutilon vitifolium* (flowering maple).

▶ *Pale-lemon and dull-white flowers will make
the border more conspicuous in twilight.*

yellow and gold borders

These are bright and dominant, especially when in strong sunlight. Plants with these radiant colours are readily seen in both the gloom of early morning and the diminishing light of evening. Yellow is therefore useful as an edging for summer-flowering bedding displays.

Flower borders

Herbaceous borders are sometimes themed as a single colour, such as yellow, but this does not mean that the border only has one colour. For example, in yellow and gold borders, yellow-and-

◄ *Plants with narrow, yellow-variegated leaves create a dramatic shape and colour constrast in a garden. Grow tender plants in pots.*

green variegated shrubs can be added to create permanency, height and complementary colour. Good yellow herbaceous perennials include *Achillea filipendulina* 'Gold Plate' (fern-leaf yarrow) with large, plate-like heads packed with deep-yellow flowers from mid- to late-summer. *Alchemilla mollis* (lady's mantle) is another superb plant, ideal for the edge of a border where it cloaks sharp, unsightly outlines.

The list of herbaceous plants for yellow borders is lengthy and includes *Coreopsis vertillata*, with bright yellow star-like flowers, dahlias, *Phlomis fruticosa* and *Verbascum bombyciferum* (mullein) – with tall flower stems and silver-haired oval leaves. Two others are *Rudbeckia fulgida* (coneflower); this has large, yellow flowers with purple-brown centres. It is superb with *Aster amellus* 'King George'. *Solidago* 'Goldenmosa' (goldenrod) bears fluffy heads of yellow flowers.

Trees and shrubs

Yellow-flowerering winter and spring trees and shrubs include *Hamamelis* (witch hazel), chimonanthus and mahonias in winter, and the glorious forsythias, *Berberis darwinii* and double-flowered gorse in spring. Many continue their display into summer, and later. Add accents of colour by grouping plants in attractive duos. Around the spreading branches of *Hamamelis mollis* (Chinese witch hazel) plant the winter-flowering *Rhododendron mucronulatum* with funnel-shaped, rose-purple flowers. For a summer leaf-colour contrast, plant the deciduous shrub *Cotinus coggygria* 'Royal Purple', with dark plum-coloured leaves.

BACKGROUND HARMONIES AND CONTRASTS

Yellow is a dramatic colour, especially when highlighted by a contrasting background. Yellow flowers look good against a white background, while lemon-coloured flowers are better suited to a red brick wall.

Climbers and wall shrubs

These range from annuals to shrubs and include the popular *Thunbergia alata*, (black-eyed Susan), a half-hardy annual raised in gentle warmth in spring before being planted in a border or against a trellis when all risk of frost has passed. Alternatively, it will scale a tripod of canes or poles. For winter colour against a wall, plant *Jasminum nudiflorum*, the winter-flowering jasmine that produces bright yellow flowers on bare stems throughout winter.

Several slightly tender shrubs benefit from being planted on the sunny side of a wall and include *Cytisus battandieri*, (Moroccan broom). During mid summer it has pineapple-scented, cone-like, golden-yellow heads of flowers amid large, grey, laburnum-like leaves. *Piptanthus nepalensis*, still better known as *Piptanthus laburnifolius* (evergreen laburnum), is also slightly tender and bears pea-shaped, bright yellow, laburnum-like flowers in late spring and early summer.

The deciduous and vigorous *Lonicera tragophylla* (Chinese woodbine) is ideal for covering archways, pergolas and walls. It produces masses of bright golden-yellow flowers from early to mid-summer.

▶ *Yellow and gold borders introduce vitality into a garden, with plants ranging from yellow-leaved border plants to glorious sunflowers.*

Key to planting

❶ *Rudbeckia fulgens* (coneflower)

❷ *Euonymus fortunei* 'Emerald 'n' Gold'

❸ *Helianthus annuus* (sunflower)

❹ *Thunbergia alata* (black-eyed Susan)

❺ *Verbascum bombyciferum* (mullein)

❻ *Achillea filipenndulina* 'Gold Plate' (fern-leaf yarrow)

❼ *Solidago* 'Goldenmosa' (golden rod)

❽ *Tagetes erecta* (African marigolds)

▲ *Gardens packed with yellow flowers and foliage are full of vitality. Hoop-like arches add interest and help to create height in a garden.*

white and silver schemes

With their brightness and purity, white flowers have a dramatic impact in strong sunlight. Silver is less dominant and is often described as greyish-white. It is less apparent because silver reflects light at many angles, whereas smooth-surfaced white petals are better reflectors of light.

Flower borders

There are many plants for grey, silver and white herbaceous borders. Those with grey and silver foliage include *Anaphalis triplinervis* (pearly everlasting) with narrow, silver-grey, lance-shaped leaves that reveal white, woolly undersides. Additionally, it bears bunched heads of white flowers during late summer. Its near relative *Anaphalis margaritacea*

◀ *Borders with white flowers and silver foliage sparkle in even the smallest amount of light, bringing unexpected vibrancy to a garden.*

yedoensis has grey leaves and heads of white flowers from mid-summer to autumn.

Many artemisias have silver-coloured leaves and none better than *Artemisia absinthium* 'Lambrook Silver', with its silvery-grey, finely divided leaves and small, round, yellow flowers during mid and late-summer. *Artemisia ludoviciana*, the white sage, has upright stems and deeply divided, woolly white leaves and silver-white flowers during late summer and early autumn. *Onopordum acanthium* (Scotch thistle) produces broad, jagged silver-grey leaves.

The range of silver-leaved plants continues with *Stachys byzantina* (lamb's tongue), with oval leaves densely covered in white, silvery hairs that create a woolly appearance. The half-hardy perennial *Senecio cineraria*, usually grown as a half-hardy annual, clothes borders with deeply lobed leaves covered in

white, woolly hairs. Herbaceous plants with white flowers include the popular *Leucanthemum maximum*, still better known as *Chrysanthemum maximum* (Shasta daisy), with masses of large, white, daisy-like flowers with yellow centres from mid- to late-summer. *Gypsophila paniculata* (baby's breath) creates clouds of white flowers amid grey-green leaves. With fewer but larger white flowers, *Romneya coulteri* (Californian tree poppy) blooms from mid-summer to autumn.

The half-hardy annual *Lobularia maritima*, better known as *Alyssum maritimum* (sweet alyssum), is ideal as an edging to summer-flowering bedding arrangements.

BACKGROUND HARMONIES AND CONTRASTS

Backgrounds suitable for white flowers are limited, and they usually look their best against a red brick wall. This colour also suits silver-coloured foliage.

Key to planting

1 *Onopordum acanthium* (Scotch thistle)

2 *Anaphalis margaritacea yedoensis*

3 *Artemisia ludoviciana* (white sage)

4 *Carpenteria californica*

5 *Wisteria sinensis* 'Alba' (white Chinese wisteria)

6 *Romneya coulteri* (Californian tree poppy)

7 *Leucanthemum maximum* (Shasta daisy)

8 *Stachys byzantina* (lamb's tongue)

Trees and shrubs

The excellent range includes *Amelanchier lamarckii* (snowy mespilus) with a mass of white flowers in spring, while *Eucryphia × nymansensis* produces 6.5cm/2⅜in-wide, white or cream flowers in late summer and early autumn. Other fine shrubs to consider are *Hydrangea arborescens* 'Grandiflora' with pure white flowers in slightly rounded heads from mid-summer to early autumn. Its relative *H. paniculata* 'Grandiflora' develops large, pyramidal, terminal heads of white flowers during late summer and autumn.

Few small-garden shrubs with white flowers are as attractive as *Magnolia stellata* (star magnolia), with 10cm/4in-wide flowers during spring. The narrow, silver-grey, willow-like leaves of *Pyrus salicifolia* 'Pendula' are also attractive, and during spring, pure white flowers appear in terminal clusters. It is best set off by blue spring-flowering bulbs. *Spiraea × arguta* (bridal wreath) and *Viburnum opulus* 'Sterile', sometimes known as *V. o.* 'Roseum', are other superb shrubs for planting in white borders.

▲ A garden seat creates an ideal pivot for this white and silver garden, and is an ideal theme for a small garden where vibrancy is desired.

▲ Plants in pots, placed on a well-drained surface, create an attractive feature and are ideal as a focal point in small gardens.

variegated foliage

Foliage with several colours never fails to attract attention, and these qualities are found in a wide range of plants from herbaceous perennials to trees, shrubs and climbers. Many have subdued colours, while others are bright and make a garden look vibrant.

Flower borders

There are more variegated herbaceous perennials than might, at first thought, be considered possible. Well-known variegated hostas include *Hosta fortunei albopicta*, *H. crispula* and *H.* 'Gold Standard'. There are many other hostas but perhaps one of the most unlikely variegated plants is *Aegopodium podagraria* 'Variegatum' (variegated ground elder). Although claimed not to be too invasive, it is best grown in large tubs where it brightens patios with light-green leaves edged with white. The perennial grass *Hakonechloa macra* 'Alboaurea' is also superb in a large tub, as well as at the corner of a raised bed. Its narrow, arching, ribbon-like leaves are variegated buff and gold, with touches of bronze.

Also ideal for borders with their vertical growth are *Iris pallida*, 'with sword-like, green and yellow striped leaves, while *I. p.* 'Argentea Variegata' has white stripes. The variegated phloxes 'Norah Leigh' and 'Harlequin' are both excellent in herbaceous borders, while *Yucca filamentosa* 'Variegata', with its sword-like leaves, always attracts attention. Give it a prominent position.

Trees and shrubs

These often create dominant displays, especially *Euonymus fortunei* 'Emerald 'n' Gold', a dense, bushy evergreen with variegated bright gold leaves; in winter they are tinged bronze-pink. 'Emerald Gaiety' and 'Harlequin' also have variegated leaves. *Aucuba japonica* 'Variegata' is also an old garden favourite with its yellow spotted green leaves creating a dominant display. It looks good in spring when surrounded by daffodils. *Elaeagnus pungens* 'Maculata' is another evergreen favourite, with stiff, leathery green leaves splashed gold.

Salvia officinalis 'Icterina' grows about 30cm/12in high and is ideal for planting beside a path, where it cloaks unsightly edges. With green and gold leaves it

◄ *This small, decorative, rail-type fence harmonizes with ornamental grasses and low-growing plants to create an attractive feature.*

forms an eye-catching feature, as does 'Tricolor', with grey-green leaves splashed creamy white, suffused with pink.

The deciduous *Cornus alba* 'Spaethii' (dogwood) has light-green leaves with irregular gold-splashed edges, with the bonus of bright red stems in winter. A near relative, *C. alternifolia* 'Argentea' is a small tree or large shrub with horizontally spreading branches bearing small green leaves with creamy white edges. Do not hide its attractive shape.

Variegated hollies have a permanent role in gardens, adding brightness throughout the year. *Ilex × altaclerensis* 'Lawsoniana' has green leaves, usually spineless, each with a central yellow splash. It bears orange-red berries in winter. *Ilex aquifolium* has many varieties with variegated, spine-edged leaves, notably 'Madame Briot' with purple stems and mottled leaves edged dark yellow.

Climbers and wall shrubs

Perhaps the best-known variegated climbers are ivies. They range from the small leaved *Hedera helix* 'Goldheart', now known as 'Oro di Bogliasco', with dark green leaves splashed yellow, to

large-leaved types. They include the variegated *H. canariensis* 'Gloire de Marengo' (Canary Island ivy), with deep green leaves and silver-grey and white variegations. There are several variegated forms of the Persian ivy; *H. colchica* 'Dentata Variegata' has leaves conspicuously edged creamy yellow, and 'Sulphur Heart' has irregular yellow splashes. *Actinidia kolomikta*, a deciduous climber, is radically different, with green leaves that develop pink-flushed white areas towards the tips.

▶ *Trailing and spreading plants help to clothe the edges of decking. Regular trimming may be necessary to prvent them becoming intrusive.*

▼ *Variegated plants soften this flight of steps and complement the distinctive tiered branches of Cornus controversa ('Variegata').*

Key to planting

1. *Hakonechloa macra* 'Alboaurea'
2. *Phlox* 'Norah Leigh'
3. *Yucca fillamentosa* 'Variegata'
4. *Cornus alternifolia* 'Argentea'
5. Variegated *phormium*
6. *Iris pallida* 'Argentea Variegata'
7. *Hosta sieboldiana* 'Frances Williams'
8. *Hosta fortunei albopicta*

mixed colour borders

There are two ways to consider 'mixed' colours: one is a medley of colours within seed-raised plants such as summer-flowering bedding plants for beds and containers. The other is planning the arrangement of individual colours and this is most dramatically achieved in the larger theatre of a garden.

Using mixed colours

In the confines of window boxes, wall baskets and hanging baskets, mixed colours within a variety are superb. For example, trailing lobelia is sold as distinct varieties in white, blue, lilac, crimson and red, but you can also grow them from mixed seed. A major practical advantage of devoting a hanging basket to a mixture of a single plant is that they will all have same degree of vigour, and none will eventually dominate its neighbour.

Mixing colours

Mixing individual colours in a garden is as much a personal preference as one of science. It is useful to use a colour wheel formed of three main colours – yellow, blue and red – and three secondaries – orange, green and violet – to reveal those that complement or harmonize.

Complementary colours are those with no common pigments, while those that harmonize share them. Consequently yellow and violet, blue and orange, and red and green are complementary, while yellow harmonizes with green and orange, blue with green and violet, and red with orange and violet.

▲ *Plants with variegated leaves create colour throughout summer and, if evergreen, the entire year. Many can be grown in pots and tubs.*

SHINY AND MATT SURFACES

The surface of a leaf influences the way it reflects light. A smooth surface reflects light at the same angle at which it is struck, and makes the light appear pure. If the surface is matt, light is reflected at different angles and creates a dull surface. In nature, however, few plant surfaces are as smooth as glass, and the scattering of light occurs from most of them.

Mixing and matching

Colour planning a garden need not involve vast areas or be expensive. Consider a corner of a shrub border, or planting an area of wall to start with.

Yellow and gold – many yellow-leaved trees and shrubs form ideal backdrops for purple-leaved plants. If the ratio of yellow to purple is about three to one they appear well-balanced. Plant the dark-leaved *Berberis thunbergii atropurpurea* with yellow-leaved shrubs like *Sambucus racemosa* 'Plumosa Aurea' (cut-leaved elder).

Key to planting

1 *Calendula officinalis* (pot marigold)

2 *Coreopsis verticillata*

3 *Cotinus coggygria* 'Notcutt's Variety'

4 *Philadelphus coronarius* 'Aureus'

5 Lupins – in mixed colours

6 *Berberis thunbergii atropurpurea*

7 *Papaver orientale*
(Oriental poppy)

8 *Geranium* 'Johnson's Blue'

Blue and purple – to create a blue background display, plant *Ceanothus* 'Cascade' against a sheltered sunny wall. It grows about 3m/10ft high and wide, and bears small, rich blue flowers in late spring and early summer; for added interest, plant the slightly tender, evergreen shrub *Choisya ternata* (Mexican orange blossom) in front of it.

Red and pink – take care when using red because it is dominant, and can be overpowering. Against a mid-green background, bright-red flowers such as the hardy annual *Papaver rhoeas* (field poppy) have a three-dimensional effect. However, most red flowers are not totally colour saturated and appear more as shades. Pink is a desaturated red and is easier to blend into a garden.

▲ *Multi-coloured hanging baskets always capture attention and invariably suit more backgrounds than those of a single colour.*

▼ *Packed borders with mixed colours are ideal features in small gardens. Remove dead flowers to encourage repeat flowering.*

apples and pears

Apples are the most popular tree fruit in temperate countries. Pears are also widely grown, but often have a temperamental nature and dessert varieties need a sunnier and more wind-sheltered position than apples. In small gardens, grow apples as cordons or espaliers.

Planting and growing apples

In the past, apple trees often grew 6m/20ft high or more, and were difficult to prune and harvest. Today, a dwarf bush apple on an M27 rootstock is ideal for a small garden, where it grows about 1.8m/6ft high and produces 5.4–7.2kg/12–16lb of fruit each year. Cordons, when grown on a similar rootstock and planted 45cm/18in apart, produce 2.2–3.1kg/5–7lb. Espaliers planted about 4.2m/14ft apart bear 9–13kg/20–30lb of fruit. Bushes demand less pruning than cordons, while espaliers need more attention.

Choose a frost-free site in full sun with shelter from strong wind. Sun is essential to ripen highly coloured dessert varieties. Apples usually flower in the early part of late spring; in areas where frosts repeatedly occur at that time, select a late-flowering variety.

Well-drained moisture-retentive soil is essential, especially for dessert varieties; culinary apple trees grow well on heavier soil. Bare-rooted trees are planted during their dormant period in winter. When planting out, mix in plenty of well-decayed garden compost or manure.

◄ *Apple trees can be grown in tubs or large pots, but ensure that only those growing on dwarf rootstocks are used.*

Container-grown trees can be planted whenever the soil is not frozen or waterlogged. Spring is best. Support cordons and espaliers with galvanized wires tensioned between strong posts 2.4–3.6m/8–12ft apart; space the wires 38–45cm/15–18in apart to about 2.1m/7ft high. Check the posts every spring for wind damage.

APPLE TREES IN TUBS

An apple tree in a container on a patio is an ideal way to grow fruit in a small garden. Dwarf rootstocks such as M27 (trees in containers grow to about 1.5m/5ft high) and M9 (up to 2.4m/8ft) make this possible, using 38cm/15in-wide wooden tubs or pots. Well-drained moisture-retentive compost is essential and in summer regular watering is needed, sometimes every day. During winter it may be necessary to wrap straw around the tub to prevent the roots freezing and getting damaged. A plastic sheet can also be used to prevent the compost from becoming too wet. Repotting every other late winter is essential, as well as feeding during summer. Large crops are not possible but good varieties to seek include 'Blenheim Orange', 'Egremont Russet', 'Spartan' and 'Sunset'.

Planting and growing pears

Unfortunately, the range of rootstocks is limited and it is not possible to grow pears on trees as dwarf as those for apples. Few gardens can accommodate pear trees up to 6m/20ft high, and therefore in small areas it is best to grow pears as cordons or espaliers. Cordon pears planted 75cm/18in apart each produce 1.8–2.7kg/4–6lb of fruit, while an espalier yields 6.8–11.3kg/15–25lb.

Planting and supporting pears is the same as for apples, but pears are more susceptible to drought than apples, so be prepared to water the soil copiously during dry periods. It is probably better to select a dessert variety of pear than a cooker but it will need a compatible pollinator that will flower at the same time. For example, 'Conference' is a partly self-fertile variety and needs other varieties, such as 'Beth' or 'Josephine de Malines'. Alternatively, if you have a warm garden plant the superb 'Doyenne du Comice', also 'Winter Nelis' (this has the bonus of keeping the fruits from late autumn to early winter).

Cordon

Single, inclined stem

Espalier

Tiered branches

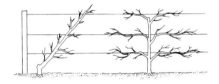

Espalier supports

Straining bolt   Tensioned wire

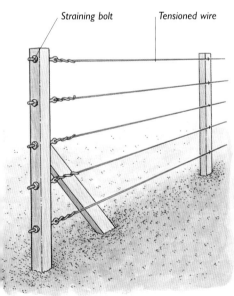

▶ *Pears grown as cordons or espaliers are ideal for planting in a small garden; the fruits are easily picked without using stepladders.*

peaches, nectarines and plums

Peaches and nectarines need a warm climate. They are closely related; nectarines are smooth-skinned sports (mutations) of peaches, which have furry skins. Nectarines are less hardy than peaches and have smaller yields. Plums are easily grown stone fruits.

Growing peaches and nectarines

In temperate countries, with the likelihood of frost in early and mid-spring and a general lack of pollinating insects at that time, it is often difficult to grow peaches and nectarines successfully.

Where conditions are least favourable, choose a peach rather than a nectarine, and always grow as a fan trained on galvanized wires against a warm, sunny, south- or south-west facing wall rather than as a bush.

Choose a reliable variety such as 'Peregrine' or 'Rochester'. Fortunately, peaches and nectarines are self-fertile.

Construct tiers of galvanized wires before planting a peach or nectarine. Position the lowest wire 30cm/1ft above the ground, with others 20cm/8in apart to a height of about 1.8m/6ft. Secure the wires 10cm/4in from the wall. Because peaches and nectarines are best grown against a wall it is essential to thoroughly prepare the soil by adding plenty of moisture-retentive, well-decayed garden compost or manure. Prepare an area 45cm/18in deep and 1m/3½ft square and position the main stem about 23cm/9in from the wall. Plant bare-rooted specimens in late autumn or early winter, and container-grown plants at any time when the soil and weather allow. Choose a two- or three-year-old plant with eight or more branches.

Rather than tying stems directly to the wires, secure them to bamboo canes, and then to the wires. The two main arms should be at an upward 45 degrees angle, with other stems spaced out.

▲ *Plant a fan-trained peach tree against a warm, sunny wall. To maintain the shape, secure the branches to tiers of galvanized wires.*

Always prune peaches and nectarines in late winter or early spring, when growth begins, but never tackle this task in winter. Initially, the purpose of pruning is to encourage the development of a fan. Pruning a two- or three-year-old plant is much easier than creating a fan from a rooted shoot with no side-shoots. On an established plant, cut back each arm of the fan by about a third, making cuts slightly above a downward pointing bud. In the following summer, shoots develop on each arm; allow three to form and tie each of them to a cane. Also, use a thumb to rub out buds growing towards the wall. During late summer, when each of these shoots is 45cm/18in long, nip out their growing points. Pick the fruit when the skin reveals a reddish flush and the flesh around the stalk softens – mid-summer to early autumn.

Growing plums

These are popular fruits. Because they flower early in the year and are vulnerable to frost, plant them in a mild, frost-free area. Dessert plums especially need a warm, sunny position to encourage good flavour. Plums can be grown in several forms, including standards, half-standards, bushes and pyramids, but in small gardens a fan-trained form is better.

Prepare the soil in the same way as for peaches and nectarines, and with a similar arrangement of tiered wires against a wall. Also, plant and prune fan-trained plants in the same way. Pick fruit from the latter part of mid-summer to late autumn, when it parts readily from the tree.

▼ Plum trees flower early in the season and therefore need a warm, sheltered position against a wall. This is an ideal form for small gardens.

Fan trained

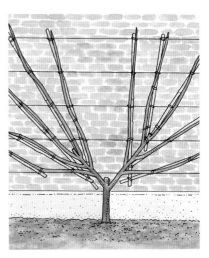

HAND POLLINATING

Peaches and nectarines flower early in the year when pollinating insects are scarce. Therefore, use a soft brush or loose ball of cotton wool to gently dab each flower every other day from the time the buds open until the petals fall.

growing soft fruits

It is surprising how many different types of soft fruits can be grown in a small garden. Raspberries grow vertically, while bushes of blackcurrants take up only a little space. Strawberries alongside paths are easily accessible, although if space is restricted they can be grown in a barrel.

Strawberries

There are several forms of these popular, easily grown fruits, including perpetual and alpine, but the summer-fruiting varietes are most widely grown. Once planted, they are usually left for three or four years before being discarded, with fresh beds prepared for new plants. It is possible to grow summer-fruiting types as an annual crop that produce high quality fruit, but it will not grow as prolifically as well-established two- or three-year-old plants. Plant bare-rooted, summer-fruiting plants between mid-summer and early autumn, and container-grown plants at any time when the soil is workable. In practice, however, they are best planted at the same time as bare-rooted plants.

Prepare strawberry beds by digging the soil in late spring or early summer, and adding well-decomposed garden compost or manure. Remove and burn perennial weeds. Just before planting, dust the surface with a general fertilizer. When planting bare-rooted plants, spread out the roots over a small mound of soil in the hole's base and check that the crown of the plant is level with the surrounding ground. Firm soil around the roots. Similarly, with container-grown plants do not bury the crown but keep it level with the soil surface. After planting, thoroughly water the soil and regularly pull up weeds.

In the following spring, sprinkle a general fertilizer around the plants, water the soil and add a mulch of straw to keep fruit off the soil. When the fruits are red all over, pick them with the calyx attached early in the morning.

Raspberries

There are two forms, summer- and autumn-fruiting, with established summer-fruiting varieties producing most fruit. Both require annual pruning.

A tiered framework of wires is essential, using strong posts (up to 3.6m/12ft apart) with galvanized wires strained between them at a height of 75cm/30cm, 1m/3½ft and 1.6m/5¼ft above ground. Plant bare-rooted canes during late autumn and early winter, or in early spring, spacing them 45cm/18in apart. Immediately after planting, cut all canes to 23–30cm/9–12in high just above a healthy bud.

During the first year, young canes develop and will fruit the following year. Pick the berries when fully coloured yet still firm.

▲ *Blackberry 'Oregon Thornless' has medium-sized fruits in late summer and early autumn and can be planted against a trellis or arch.*

Blackcurrants

They are borne on deciduous bushes for picking during the latter part of mid-summer and late summer. Position each plant slightly deeper than usual to allow for soil settlement and encourage the development of shoots from below. Space plants 1.5m/5ft apart, and cut all stems to about 2.5cm/1in above the surface. Plant young, container-grown bushes at any time of the year when the soil and weather allow. If planted in summer, wait until autumn and cut out all the old shoots to soil level. Prune autumn to spring planting immediately.

STRAWBERRIES IN BARRELS

For more than 100 years strawberries have been grown in wooden barrels with holes cut in their sides. Good drainage is essential. Drill drainage holes in the barrel's base, add clean rubble and place a 10–15cm/4–6in-wide wire-netting tube filled with drainage material in the centre. Fill the barrel with well-drained compost, and put a strawberry plant into each hole.

▲ Growing strawberries in pots is popular in small gardens, especially as it is a way to prevent slugs and snails damaging the fruits.

Planting strawberries

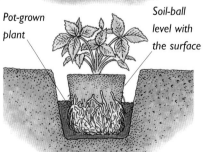

Spread out the roots over a small mound

Bare-rooted plant

Pot-grown plant

Soil-ball level with the surface

Planting blackcurrants

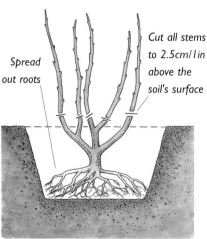

Spread out roots

Cut all stems to 2.5cm/1in above the soil's surface

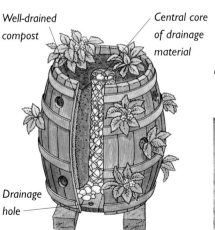

Well-drained compost

Central core of drainage material

Drainage hole

vegetables for small gardens

Some vegetables, such as asparagus and globe artichokes, are perennials and once established continue producing crops for several years. Others are sown each year and are rotated around a vegetable plot to ensure that they produce the best possible crops.

Salad crops

These are popular and easily grown; there are many interesting and colourful varieties to choose from.

❁ Outdoor cucumbers – also known as ridge cucumbers, are easily grown in fertile, moisture-retentive soil. They are best grown in a warm, sunny position sheltered from cold wind.

In mid-spring dig a hole 30cm/12in deep and wide. Fill it with a mixture of

◀ *Vegetables can be grown in even the smallest garden and often close together. Where possible, choose moderately vigorous varieties.*

equal parts of top-soil and well-decayed garden compost or manure, and make a mound of soil on the surface. In late spring or early summer, sow three seeds 18mm/¾in deep and 5cm/2in apart. Water and cover them with a large jam-jar. Water regularly and after germination remove the cover. Later, pull up the two weakest seedlings. When side-shoots have five or six leaves, pinch out their tips to just beyond a leaf joint. Water plants regularly, and feed them when the first fruits start to swell.

❁ Lettuces – these are popular, with a wide range of types. They include Butterheads (cabbage-type, with large, soft, smooth-edged leaves); Crispheads (another cabbage-type, with rounded heads and curled and crisp leaves; Cos lettuces (upright growth and oblong heads); Loose-leaf lettuces (masses of loose, wavy-edged leaves that are picked individually).

By sowing seeds at various times, lettuces can be harvested throughout most of the year, though summer-sown lettuces are the easiest to grow. From mid-spring to the early part of late summer, sow seeds thinly and evenly in 12mm/½in deep drills 25cm/10in apart. Keep the area moist. When seedlings are about 2.5cm/1in high, thin them first to 10cm/4in apart and later to 30cm/12in. Thin small varieties to 25cm/10in apart. From the latter part of early summer to autumn harvest the lettuces.

❁ Radishes – from mid-spring to late summer, sow seeds evenly and thinly every two weeks. Form drills 12mm/½in deep and 15cm/6in apart. Germination takes five to seven days and when the seedlings are large enough to handle, thin them to 2.5cm/1in apart. Re-firm the soil around them and water it. Harvest the radishes when they are young. If left, they become woody.

❁ Spring onions – in addition to bulbing types, there are spring onions, also known as salad onions and bunching onions, that are delicious in salads.

TOMATOES ON A PATIO

To grow tomatoes successfully choose a sheltered, sunny position, preferably in front of a south-facing wall. On a patio they can be grown in large pots or in a growing bag. When they are grown in pots the tall stems will need to be supported with bamboo canes, but for tomato plants in a growing bag, a proprietary supporting framework is better. Plant two tomato plants in a standard-size bag. There are two types of tomato plants: cordon and bush. Cordon types produce side-shoots which must be snapped off when young, while bush tomatoes do not require this treatment. When cordon tomatoes have produced four trusses of fruits, pinch out the shoot at two leaves above the top truss. Water and feed plants regularly throughout the summer and pick the fruit as it ripens.

Growing bag

Keep the compost moist

Water the root-ball before planting

▲ Radish 'Sparkler', a variety with globular roots, is quick and easy to grow. Sow seeds evenly and thinly.

▼ Vegetable gardens can be decorative and with plenty of eye-appeal. Vegetables can also be grown alongside flowers in cottage gardens.

growing herbs in small gardens

Several herbs, such as the biennial angelica, are large and dominant – and best planted in herbaceous or large herb borders. Most herbs though, are suitable for small gardens, while prostrate types can be planted between paving slabs arranged in a chessboard pattern.

MAKING A HERB CARTWHEEL

Dig the soil, removing perennial weeds and, if necessary, mix in well-decayed garden compost to assist water retention. Firm the soil evenly, then rake level.

Tie the ends of a 90cm/3ft-long piece of string to two canes and insert one in the bed's centre. Use the other end to scribe a circle 1.8m/6ft in diameter. Place small pebbles in a 25–30cm/10–12in-wide circle in the centre, and larger pebbles around the perimeter.

Mark the positions of the spokes with more pebbles, creating 'triangles' about 38cm/15in wide at the base. Water the plants in their containers the day before planting, then, still in their pots, arrange them in the cartwheel in an attractive design. Plant them out, thoroughly water the soil and, for greater colour, cover the soil with coloured gravels.

Cartwheel herb gardens

These are ornamental and functional features that can be tailored to fit areas only 1.8m/6ft square. Preferably, an old cartwheel is needed, but simulated designs are easily created by using large pebbles to indicate the circumference and spokes.

Chessboard designs

This is a novel way to grow low-growing herbs. Select an area, perhaps 2.28m/7½ft square, and prepare the soil as for a cartwheel garden. Then lay 45cm/18in-square paving slabs in a chessboard arrangement leaving alternate squares uncovered. Plant the uncovered squares with a selection of low-growing herbs. Where herbs do not completely cover the soil, spread pea shingle or stone chippings over the soil. This will look attractive and reduce moisture loss.

▼ *Herb wheels, closely planted with segments of contrasting thymes, create an attractive and easy-to-manage feature.*

Nine popular herbs

Balm – herbaceous perennial with lemon-scented green leaves.

Caraway – biennial with fern-like leaves and umbrella-like heads of green flowers.

Chives – bulbous, with tubular leaves and rose-pink flowers.

Dill – hardy annual with blue-green leaves and umbrella-like heads of yellow flowers.

Fennel – herbaceous perennial with blue-green leaves and golden-yellow flowers in large, umbrella-like heads.

Mint – herbaceous perennial with invasive roots. Wide range, from spearmint to apple mint.

Parsley – biennial, with crinkled or flat (more strongly flavoured) green leaves.

Sage – short-lived shrub, with grey-green leaves and spires of violet-blue flowers in early summer. There are forms with more ornamental leaves (purple, and some variegated) but they are mainly used to create colour in borders.

Thyme – low-growing, shrubby perennial. Garden thyme is a superb culinary herb, but additionally there are those with coloured leaves that add colour to chessboard designs.

▼ *Enhance herb gardens by positioning small and low-growing herbs in spaces left when paving slabs are laid in a chessboard pattern.*

HERBS IN CONTAINERS

Small herbs are ideal grown in window boxes. A variety of low-growing herbs can be grown in troughs and arranged along the edge of a patio, verandah or balcony.

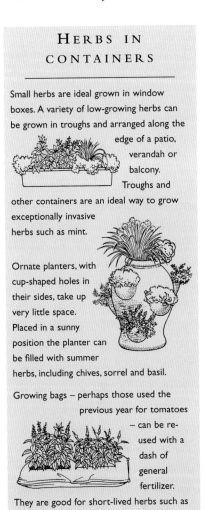

Troughs and other containers are an ideal way to grow exceptionally invasive herbs such as mint.

Ornate planters, with cup-shaped holes in their sides, take up very little space. Placed in a sunny position the planter can be filled with summer herbs, including chives, sorrel and basil.

Growing bags – perhaps those used the previous year for tomatoes – can be re-used with a dash of general fertilizer.

They are good for short-lived herbs such as parsley.

greenhouse gardening

Greenhouses add a further dimension to gardening, and enable a wider range of plants to be grown. Summer-flowering bedding plants can be sown in gentle warmth in late winter and early spring, for later planting in borders and containers when all risk of frost has passed.

Range of greenhouses

Greenhouses range in shape, structure and size giving a very wide choice. Where possible, choose the largest greenhouse you can afford that will fit into your garden. Growing plants in greenhouses often becomes a passion demanding ever more space.

❀ Even-span – also known as full-span, have a traditional outline with a ridged sloping glass roof. Traditionally made of wood, they have a low brick or wood-panelled base and glass above. Wooden designs are still available but aluminium types are increasingly popular; these have glass from the ground to the apex.

❀ Even-span greenhouses about 2.4m/8ft wide have a central path, and 90cm/3ft-wide areas on both sides that can be used for staging or growing plants such as tomatoes at ground level. Where a greenhouse is 1.8m/6ft or 2.1m/7ft wide the spaces will be smaller but still thoroughly practical.

❀ Lean-to – these are designed in width and length to suit the wall they are constructed against. Most lean-to greenhouses are glazed from soil level to the top, but when given a brick surround to about 75cm/2½ft high they begin to look like a conservatory, especially where there is direct entry into the house.

❀ Hexagonal – these have a more modern design and are becoming increasingly popular. Invariably they are constructed of aluminium with glass. Staging can be bought to fit.

❀ Mini types – even small gardens can have a greenhouse, providing it is tiny. They have a lean-to nature and can be

◄ *Wood-framed lean-to greenhouses are ideal for mature and informal gardens. Aluminium-framed types have a rather more clinical nature.*

positioned against a garden wall, stout fence or the house. Proprietary staging is available and young plants can be raised in them in spring. However, because the volume of air is small, dramatic fluctuations in temperature can occur when the front is closed.

Wood or metal?

Greenhouses were traditionally constructed of wood but increasingly aluminium is now used.

✹ Timber – the type of wood markedly influences its longevity. Baltic red wood, also known as yellow deal, is used but needs regular painting. Western red cedar is more durable and, instead of being painted, is regularly coated in linseed oil.

The Victorians used long-lasting oak and teak, but nowadays their high cost usually makes them prohibitively expensive.

✹ Aluminium – this is widely used and, when glass is added, creates a strong structure. The extruded aluminium is designed so that both shelving and insulation brackets can be attached. Additionally, because the glazing bars are narrower than those of wood, much more light enters the greenhouse.

▶ *Aluminium-framed greenhouses are available in many interesting shapes, including a wigwam (right) and a hexagonal shape.*

▼ *The all-glass, aluminium-framed greenhouse enables the maximum amount of light to enter the structure.*

POSITIONING A GREENHOUSE

Choosing the right position in a garden for a greenhouse can reduce fuel bills. Try to:

✹ Position full-span greenhouses so that the span runs east-to-west. But with lean-to types, put them against a south- or west-facing wall.

Where possible, position doors on the side away from the prevailing wind. If the door is hinged ensure that it does not open directly into the wind; similarly, if it slides, check that it first opens on the side away from the prevailing wind.

✹ Avoid positions under overhanging trees which block out light; a snapping branch could also cause damage.

✹ Because strong winds in late winter and early spring soon cool a greenhouse, plant an evergreen hedge several metres/yards away on the north or windward side.

Index

PICTURE CREDITS
Liz Eddison/Designer: Artisan Landscape Company, Tatton Park 2000 51r/David Brum, Hampton Court 2000 74b, 206b/Chelsea 2000 37bl/Designer: Julian Dowle 27/Designer: Kevin Dunne, Tatton Park 2000/Designer: Alison Evans, Tatton Park 2000 17t/Designer: Guy Farthing, Hampton Court 2000 29/Designer: Alan Gardner, Hampton Court 2000 21/Designer: Carol Klein 10b, 77b/Designer: Lindsay Knight, Chelsea 2000 33/Designer: Land Art, Hampton Court 2000 16-17b, 28b/Designer: Natural & Oriental Water Garden 52/Designer: Room in the Garden 37t/Designer: Alan Sargent, Chelsea 1999 31t Chelsea 2000 12, 20b, 53/Designer: Paul Stone 38b/Designer: Michael Upward & Richard Mercer 65/Designer: Pamela Woods, Hampton Court 1999 75; Neil Holmes 83, 86, 66b; Harry Smith Collection 51l, 84, 85; David Squire 59, 63.